FACE TO [FACE WITH]
FIDEL CASTRO

FACE TO FACE WITH
FIDEL CASTRO

A conversation with
Tomás Borge

Translated by Mary Todd

OCEAN

Cover design by David Spratt

ISBN 1-875284-72-9

First edition, 1993

Printed in Australia

Published by Ocean Press
GPO Box 3279, Melbourne, Victoria 3001, Australia

Distributed in the USA by the Talman Company,
131 Spring Street, New York, NY 10012, USA
Distributed in Britain and Europe by Central Books
99 Wallis Road, London E9 5LN, Britain
Distributed in Australia by Astam Books
162-8 Parramatta Road, Stanmore, NSW 2048, Australia

Contents

This book was originally published in Cuba in August 1992 as *Un grano de maíz* [A kernel of corn] by the Office of Publications of the Council of State. The interview with Fidel Castro by Tomás Borge took place between April 18-20, 1992.

Tomás Borge was Minister of the Interior in the Sandinista government in Nicaragua between 1979-90. He is the only surviving founder of the Sandinista National Liberation Front (FSLN) of Nicaragua. Borge is also a distinguished poet and writer.

Introduction

I

I approached Fidel Castro in a critical spirit, with a sense of history and renewed faith in the values that, for those who have become disenchanted in recent times, have become obsolete and bothersome.

I chose the form of an interview because I was convinced that I should ask the Cuban leader questions that had occurred to me and that other political leaders had asked me or that I had heard from those who live in back alleys.

Of those questions, the most important one — because it is asked in all forums, from university groups to businessmen's breakfasts — is whether or not socialism disappeared with the collapse of the Soviet Union and the socialist camp per se.

In the midst of the present ideological hullabaloo, which has given rise to excessive euphoria in some and to unbearable wailing in others, Cuba — pressured by the changes in world geopolitics, victimized by an Olympic disinformation campaign and subjected to a tighter blockade than any other country in the history of the world — is the object of such bleak prognostications.

Even the friends of the Cuban Revolution — who are more than is generally believed — express doubts about the final judgment, though many of us are still firmly convinced that Cuba will emerge victorious from the battle.

Cubans say they will continue to open up broad paths, pooling their efforts, pulling out the weeds and (without fanfare) rectifying mistakes.

As I saw on my recent visits to the island, Fidel and his comrades have a contagious, enthusiastic belief that this over-

1

whelming period is transitory, like an insolent storm cloud that blots out the light of the sun for a short time.

II

Some maintain that the in-many-ways heartrending events that took place in the Soviet Union and the other Eastern European countries haven't meant the defeat of socialism, that so-called real socialism is no more than an episode rather similar to the Paris Commune, when the workers tried to storm the heavens.

That historic experience was the source from which the classics of Marxism inferred the maxim of the worker-farmer alliance. Likewise, the causes of this disaster should be studied so the conclusions to be drawn from them may contribute to a social project that is even more closely identified with the dreams of men and women.

Real socialism, with its great achievements in health, education, housing and employment, was far from being a society decked out in panther skins and goldfinch feathers, a society of radiant smiles and free creation or one of prodigious dialectics between science and production — the society we expect of socialism without any adjectives.

With the overthrow of the monoliths of dogmatism, bureaucracy and authoritarianism and with the divorce between the masses and reality, humanity has won the right to search for the keys to earthly paradise, which have been lost in some convolution of political strategy.

Socialism is the creation of the new human being, the citizen of the 21st century: a person repelled by routine and arrogance; who understands freedom to be something inherent to revolution; and who is the enemy of schemata and the lover of heresy, a critic and a dreamer.

Once, I said that we should believe in saints who urinated and in the mortality of dogmas and cling to the utopia of a fraternal, smart human race. If this weren't possible, life wouldn't have much point... Utopias can be achieved.

III

This wasn't the first time I had visited the place where Fidel Castro spends a large part of his time. Several members of the national leadership of the Sandinista National Liberation Front (FSLN) had been there prior to the victory of the Nicaraguan Revolution, taking part in a lively 12-hour discussion in the course of which we drank a barrel of coffee and inhaled a ton of nicotine.

Frequently, we talked to dawn. On one occasion, he talked to me about his boundless confidence in human beings, and we were saddened when we spoke of the weaknesses, grudges, envy and ambitions that frequently surrounded political leaders.

I don't notice nuances very much, so I asked my wife, Marcela Pérez Silva — who, together with Margarita Suzán, my assistant, carried our impressive load of tapes and films — to describe the ambience when the long-awaited ceremony began.

Havana under Fidel's window is beautiful. Its tree-lined streets can be seen over the shoulder of the flood-lit, solemn statue of Martí that stands in Revolution Square.

From the window, we could see the city; inside the room, we saw all of Cuba. It was 2:00 a.m. on Sunday morning.

We reached Fidel's office after passing through rooms filled with delicate ferns and fan-like palm trees that expert, loving hands have miraculously managed to adapt to life indoors. (People say it was Celia Sánchez who wove these green traceries and that her spirit is still there, in the heart of one of her many orchids.)

Fidel's office is large and friendly. A portrait of Camilo Cienfuegos smiles down on visitors from the brick wall, looking off to one side from under his wide-brimmed hat. The office is filled with fresh-cut flowers and is furnished with soft chairs propitious for meetings. A desk stands at right angles to a wooden bookshelf on which the most fantastic objects coexist in absolute anarchy: manuals of biogenetics, mother-of-pearl

shells that give back the sound of the sea, books of
ancient history, treatises on irrigation, a maté gourd with
a silver tube that makes me think it was Che's, a Bible, a
biography of Fidel in English, a pre-Columbian sculpture,
a beautiful but worn collection of world classics, a little
magic box that records the birth of each child in Cuba and
in the world, and a letter in Bolívar's handwriting. Farther
away is a long, heavy work table with many chairs. Many
feverish early morning sessions of discussions and
decisions have taken place around it. Outside, the city
lights were like a carpet of tiny stars.

Fidel was standing, with stars and laurel leaves on his
shoulders — shoulders on which doves alight.

The Commanders sat down in front of the window,
facing each other. They looked like priests about to
officiate. The air was as clear as crystal. Tomás's opening
words established another time, in which all periods
blended. He asked, proposed and provoked responses. He
unleashed memories, seas and storms. Fidel replied in a
voice of thunder, and his words evoked images — of the
victorious builders of utopia, carrying lighted torches and
holding children by the hand, or of a white horse
galloping past, its mane blowing in the wind. Meanwhile,
Fidel moved around, filling the room like a mountain,
recalling the battles won and those yet to be waged.

The confidences continued for two days after this
early morning session. When the interview came to an
end, the sun was rising for the third time. Before turning
off my tape recorder, I looked toward the window. The
light was tenuous, but I could clearly see Martí, as if he
had come to look at Cuba over Fidel's shoulder.

IV

Fidel's concept of democracy and the possibility of changes in the
political structure in Cuba were two of the main topics we took

up in this interview, which was held in three sessions, with a total of 10 hours of taping, starting on April 18.

I also questioned the Cuban leader about the prospects of the revolutionary struggle in Latin America and other parts of the Third World. I asked for his opinions of Stalin and Gorbachev and also asked about his literary and other likes.

His views on the much-argued-about anniversary of Columbus's arrival at our coasts — triumphant for Europeans but heartrending for the native peoples of the Americas — form another important chapter.

Of all that Fidel says here, I was particularly impressed by his persuasive dissertation, an anthological poem, on Cuba's respect for human rights and his reflections on humanity, the human condition and human beings as the protagonists in the inconstancy of history.

This interview is not impartial; it clings to life after the recent funeral rites, seeking to light a spark in the dark. In my efforts to do this, I had to delve into Fidel Castro's incredible memory and singular intelligence.

If I have achieved this purpose, I will feel compensated for everything life has dealt me since the Sandinista reversal, the collapses and the monotonous sound of the trumpet that indecently announces the perpetuity of liberalism and the end of utopias.

This conversation with Fidel has reaffirmed my convictions and given me more arguments for my enthusiasm for solidarity and for taking the measure of the affront to the intelligence and honor of human beings.

I hope that the peoples of Latin America and other parts of the world will find this dialogue a stimulus to reflection and encouragement to preserving their hope in causes that have never ceased to be legitimate. We won't return to the mountains again, but we are confident that, with our faith, the mountains will return to us.

This interview with Fidel has helped me by confirming the need for the self-criticism that, as political leaders, we have engaged in — or are obliged to engage in — in every reversal and in the shadows.

The rest is a journalistic exercise, an entertaining illustration — even a literary pleasure.

Tomás Borge
Managua, June 1, 1992

CHAPTER 1

History and posterity

As always, Fidel — wearing an olive green uniform — was in good humor, hyperactive.

Some nights earlier, I had dreamed that his beard was a special, indefinable color, and I was almost surprised to find it just as white as I'd remembered. I imagine he's already been told that his sparkling eyes have an affectionate, direct glance. He was a little thinner and looked a little younger.

Yesterday, Saturday, when we visited people harvesting potatoes, tomatoes and eggplant, that fervor and so many demonstrations of courage and love impressed me greatly. Later on, at 1:00 a.m., when we greeted close to 300 representatives of Latin America and the Caribbean, their expressions of solidarity were clearly etched in my mind.

Today, Sunday, at this unusual hour, my first temptation was to ask Fidel about the origins of that growing vitality even in the midst of so many difficulties. I didn't ask him, however, because I was sure that the main reason why the man in front of me moved with the energy of a thoroughbred lay in the needs and dramas of every day. I know that challenges increase his vitality.

For some years, I've been free of the inhibitions that his presence caused in me at first; however, I felt inhibited again in this special context. I remembered that we had talked for hours here on different topics, from human splits to intimate conflicts. At one time, we'd had a long conversation about power, and I was going to ask him some questions about power during this conversation, too.

This time, I was approaching him as a journalist, with the role of stirring him up, asking subversive questions, seeking a new response. This time, I wasn't supposed to be a partner; I hoped that I would be

7

able to handle this situation, which was so strange for me — and, my friend, to play the difficult role of devil's advocate.

T. B.

Tomás Borge: You know something about this impressive flood of light that surrounds you, Fidel, and you accept it, aware that it belongs to history more than to any human being in this period of history. What do you feel, now that your immortality is assured?

Fidel Castro: Before answering your question, I, too, should make a small introduction. First of all, I have listened to your words with great interest; really, I marvel at them, at your capacity of expression and the beautiful way you say things, the poetic way you speak. They say that a poet is born and an orator, made. I made myself into an orator of sorts. You are still a better speaker than I. You have the advantage of being both a born poet and a born orator. I am not a born poet, but I became an orator.

Moreover, I appreciate the kindness of your words, as impartial as they may be.

You said that you were going to try to overcome some inhibitions and work as a journalist. You even recalled other times when we had talked, and you said you felt inhibited, but I think that, in this case, my position is harder than yours. The fact that there are ties of great friendship, trust, understanding, affection and great respect between us makes my role much more difficult than yours. When an enemy journalist interviews me, I argue a lot, respond with energy, attack and counterattack, but it will be very difficult for me to act this way with you, a journalist who is a friend, even if you ask questions that are much harder than the ones any other journalist may put to me. Here, I'm not talking about a journalist who is either friendly or unfriendly, but simply a journalist. In your case, two circumstances are indivisible: you are both a journalist and a friend. Therefore, I would like to make it clear that I'm the one who is faced with a very challenging test.

I will try to come through this experience with flying colors, to answer your questions to the best of my ability, to tell you as much as possible and omit as little as possible, and I hope that we will achieve the best possible atmosphere for an interview of this kind.

I've had some rather similar interviews, with people with whom I didn't have so many ties of friendship as I have with you. That, for example, was the case with Frei Betto, who asked me a lot of questions of another kind right there where you're sitting. We talked for hours, and we managed to create an atmosphere of intimacy and of conversation; he asked me some quite difficult questions. I don't expect that your questions will be at all easy, which makes my participation in this conversation even more difficult, since I feel duty-bound to reply in a satisfactory manner.

Tomás Borge: Immortality is somewhat troublesome, like love that is a victim of the mist, perhaps something about which it's better not to think.

Fidel Castro: Now I can try to answer your question. You wanted to know how someone feels who thinks they have a place in history.

That question is difficult to answer — first of all, because I haven't stopped to think about this kind of thing very often; I've meditated very little about this. And, even admitting that I do have some small place in the history of this era in which I've lived, I have my own criteria about history, about what history is or can be.

Sometimes I wonder if true history really exists, because history is the object of so many and such diverse interpretations and points of view that it is sometimes hard to be sure that there is such a thing as true history. It seems to me that the most that can be created is an approximation of the events in the lives of a person and people, not a truly objective history of any person or people.

I've always liked history a lot, practically since I began to be able to reason. I think everybody likes history. I don't think there are any children who don't like stories. If you say to a child, "I'm going to tell you a story," they will stop what they're doing to listen.

They even say that once, when Demosthenes was in the

public square giving a philippic, an important political speech, and nobody was paying him any attention, he told them, "Listen, because I'm going to tell you a story," and everybody immediately paid attention. This simply shows that everybody likes history in one form or another.

I like it very much indeed. All my life, I've read all the history I could — all that my busy life left time for. This was both as a young man and later, as a university student, in my life before the Revolution, during the Revolution, in jail, in exile and throughout these years since the triumph of the Revolution, when I've always managed to take some time from sleep or from work — one hour, or two or three, and sometimes more — for reading. Naturally, I read all kinds of things, from all kinds of books, but I've always had a special liking for historical works. I have read so many that I'm able to question the events the books are about. This is why I say that the histories we know are approximations. That's the first thing.

Secondly, I don't think history has been impartial very often; frequently, it has become confused with legend. When I read the things that are said about important figures of ancient times and try to learn what the sources for that information were, I often find that there was only one source. There were just a few Greek and Roman historians who spoke of great episodes of antiquity, and sometimes there are very few sources for what they relate. I'm very sorry that so many books of ancient history, so many of those early histories that were written and preserved in the famous library of Alexandria, were burned during the battle that took place there between Julius Caesar and his adversaries some years before the birth of Christ. It's a shame that so many books that would have provided us with information about ancient times were lost.

Throughout history, those who more or less successfully wrote history often contributed a large dose of legend, fantasy and subjectivism. Thus, you can't be sure about the objectivity of history.

Tomás Borge: Do you think that this distrust of historical objectivity has influenced very recent events?

Fidel Castro: Yes, even recent events. I can see this with regard to our own struggle for liberation in the Sierra Maestra mountains. I have a lot of documents and other materials and I remember an infinity of things about that whole period, especially many basic ideas and concepts, and I've seen the testimonies of many comrades who have written about those events. I haven't been able to give my version of those things yet, but I can see that many details of what is described — and some of these accounts have been written well, even brilliantly — in these very interesting and valuable testimonies still reflect ignorance of the overall concept of the war, strategy, and other basic, essential ideas that guided events. Often, the writers limit themselves to describing events in which they participated directly, what happened to them each day, what news they heard, what vision they had of what happened that day, using a very incomplete approach.

Other comrades were very close to the leadership. Juan Almeida, for example, has written some excellent things about the war of liberation. They contain a lot of information, because he asked questions of many witnesses and many protagonists in those events, creating texts that I've read with admiration. But I've also read many other things that comrades have written in very good faith that reflect incomplete views.

In addition, I've noted that everyone who writes something tends to concentrate on their own experiences and their own part in events. Sometimes, when I think that now, over 30 years later, those of us who participated most directly in the initial stages of that war and made the main decisions haven't yet written our version of what happened, it makes me afraid that incomplete views of those events may be all that will remain.

If — 40, 50 or 100 years from now — historians begin to search for sources of what happened in that period of history in Cuba, what will they write? How close will they come to the facts, and how far away from them will they be? I'm speaking of history as something that reflects the truth, with the greatest possible objectivity.

Tomás Borge: When are you going to write your own version?

Fidel Castro: My friend, the more bitter I get with all the things I see... But I also have some people here who have collected historical facts, have worked in the archives; these people know a lot more than I do about everything I did; therefore, I wouldn't have to do more than give them some basic ideas.

I've thought about writing first about the offensive, beginning with the days of the enemy offensive and our counteroffensive, which were decisive moments, when there were many battles and much fighting. I could tell the history of the war, which would be not so much my version as that of the team of people who would work on it, because they have gathered many testimonies and done many things that I haven't been able to do.

I could illustrate what happened at each moment with examples of strategy, concepts and ideas and say why we did one thing at one time and something else at another. I could explain why we engaged in each of those movements, why we adopted each tactic and what strategy we followed. The war lasted 25 months, and I was there with the troops every day for all that time — no, I left them on one day, December 24, 1958, when I went to see my mother in Birán. We controlled nearly all of the territory, and I went with two jeeps, around 12 men and a few machine guns. That was the only day I left on personal business.

Tomás Borge: This is the first time anybody's heard of that, Fidel.
Fidel Castro: Well, that isn't very important. I went to see her, and I came back, traveling all night; I spent the day with her and came back at night. It was December 24; I returned for the operations in many different places. We were fighting; we had the Bayamo army along a long line at our rear, but we'd already defeated the troops.

The history of the war is very interesting. Starting with the 15 men who regrouped, we went on to destroy Batista's army — he had 80,000 men under arms — in 24 months. Organizing our small army again, starting from scratch, growing, and emerging victorious was a notable achievement. It helped me to think a lot and to read many books about Cuba's war of independence against Spain, so as to learn from the strategy and tactics of the Mambí army and Mambí leaders and get an idea of how to fight.

But, going back to your first question... Sometimes we use the term "history" in a certain way, as when we say that history will prove us right. I myself used it in that sense during the trial for the attack on the Moncada Garrison when I said, "History will absolve me." That was an expression of confidence in the future, an expression of confidence in the ideas I was defending as the fairest ones and of the cause I was defending as the most honorable one. I meant that the future would recognize this because, in the future, those ideas would be made realities; in the future, people would know everything about what happened: what we did and what our adversaries did, what goals we sought and what goals our adversaries sought, and who was right — we or the judges who were trying us, who had acted dishonestly in discharging a public trust, who had abandoned their oath of loyalty to the Constitution and were serving a tyrannical regime. I was challenging them, absolutely convinced that the ideas we were defending would triumph in our homeland someday — a conviction I still have, that humanity's legitimate causes will always advance and triumph eventually.

Tomás Borge: Then history will never be written with absolute objectivity?

Fidel Castro: This confidence I have expressed and this expression of faith in the future I have made don't imply certainty that some day history must be written with absolute objectivity. In the times in which we live, there is a science that is arrayed against history: the science of publicity, propaganda, disinformation and lies, the science of calumny, in which our adversaries take the prize.

Tomás Borge: Many things have been said about Cuba...

Fidel Castro: In your introduction, you spoke of the things that have been said in one sense or another. I think that no other historical process at any time was ever subjected to as much false propaganda as has been launched about the Cuban Revolution and the protagonists in the Cuban Revolution.

Our adversaries have tried to write history ahead of time, to fabricate conclusions and legends before the fact. I would say,

Tomás, that the peoples' instinct and ability to distinguish the true from the false have defended and helped us more than the resources we had with which to counter that avalanche of publicity and imperialism's campaign against Cuba. If this weren't so, there wouldn't be any explanation for the reactions so many people in the world have to the Cuban Revolution, in spite of the incessant, ever increasing deluge of negative publicity and the negative campaign that is being waged against the Cuban Revolution — a campaign that is now being mounted on a larger scale than ever before, especially since the collapse of the socialist camp. Imperialism was left with practically just one enemy — Cuba — and all of that enormous apparatus, all those immense resources that used to be directed against the entire socialist community, against the Soviet Union and all of the other socialist countries, are now directed almost exclusively against Cuba. Nevertheless, even at this time, there is a tremendous, extraordinary reaction of solidarity with our country.

Tomás Borge: How can you explain this thing, that seems a miracle?

Fidel Castro: How can you explain it if you can't talk with each and every one of those people, if you can't send them a message? It's as if they had enough enlightenment, enough instinct, to recognize the truth in the midst of that barrage that has confused so many people, including many intellectuals. Yet it doesn't confuse the simple people, the noble people, many worthy individuals in Latin America and the rest of the world who can see, in the midst of that sea of lies and propaganda, at least a part of the truth, or the essence of the truth, and manage to understand the great merit of the extraordinary, heroic struggle that our people are waging against the enemies of humanity, the enemies of human progress, the enemies of human rights, the enemies of the peoples' future, the world's plunderers par excellence, the symbols of oppression and exploitation. It's as if people had antennae or something else for distinguishing between what is true and what is false.

How much time must pass before, basing itself on the objective facts, posterity will be able to pass impartial judgment on everything that has happened regarding Cuba, the Cuban Revolution and the role of the leaders in that Revolution? Nobody can say. If a wave of reaction should prevail for a long time in the world, that reaction would write the history; the oppressors and aggressors would be the ones to write history. Later on, though, another wave would certainly come — a progressive, revolutionary wave of change in favor of humanity, and that would be the time for rewriting that history in an objective way.

As I see it, no matter what the facts are, there are interpretations of the facts.

I should tell you something that forms part of my thinking, of what I believe. I believe that a revolutionary, a fighter who is involved in the sphere of politics, in the sphere of a revolution, cannot think about glory or history. I'm entirely convinced of this.

Tomás Borge: Nevertheless, some people have been obsessed with history...

Fidel Castro: I know of many people, great figures, who were obsessed with glory and history. Among these great figures, for example, there was Napoleon Bonaparte. Every speech, proclamation, statement and letter of his spoke of glory and his role in history; he worried about that sort of thing all the time. Napoleon was a revolutionary — with his armies, he spread the ideas of the French Revolution throughout Europe. Later on, he changed and thought more about the empire and the crown and allied himself with the aristocracy or developed a new form of aristocracy. But, unquestionably, he played an important role in history and especially in spreading the ideas of the French Revolution.

Bolívar was another man who thought about history a lot — though, of course, he was very different from Napoleon and, in my view, incomparably superior to him. I've read a great deal about Bolívar, and I never tire of reading about him, about all of his experiences, his tragedies and his successes. I have tremendous fellow feeling for Bolívar, which I don't have for any other figure in history — I'm talking about the great figures in history — but he was excessively concerned with history; he tormented himself thinking about history and how posterity would view and judge him.

In our era, in which you can have a slightly broader view — "broader", I'm not going to say "exact" — a more complete view of what has happened and a different approach to and view of the role of human beings, concern with history wouldn't be compatible with the duty of a revolutionary, the selflessness every revolutionary should have, their total dedication. I think that a revolutionary should give everything for the cause, be ready to pay whatever price may be necessary for a specific objective, for the triumph of an idea or a cause, and shouldn't worry about themselves. Concern about yourself can have a destructive influence on a person's conduct. In short, I can't see how you can justify it in today's world, because nobody has the right to fight for glory or to fight to make an impression on posterity. Do you see? It would be selfish to do that.

Tomás Borge: From what I hear, you aren't concerned about history...

Fidel Castro: I've always thought this way, so I haven't had that concern, being tortured by what people think of me. That's something I don't feel I have the right to concern myself about. It's as if you were to fight a battle without seeking to achieve a goal — as if we'd fought at the Bay of Pigs not to defend our country's integrity, sovereignty and independence and not to defend the Revolution but to chalk up a great military triumph, to go down in history with a great military victory, the first victory scored against imperialism. Is any person's glory worth bloodshed?

When I remember all the battles — the tremendous battles — we fought in the Sierra Maestra and the efforts and sacrifices we asked the combatants to make, trying to free our country of the tyranny and to advance the Revolution, it's clear that we couldn't have been thinking about our own merits and personal glory for even a second at the cost of the sacrifices made by so many people. For me, image was secondary, because it didn't seem honest to me to ask for an atom of sacrifice from others for the purpose of having that sacrifice result in glory, in improving my image.

Tomás Borge: Some say, however, that one of the purposes of Cuba's military presence in Africa was to win laurels.

Fidel Castro: I also remember our internationalist missions, including the one in Angola, and those who placed their lives in danger, the difficult operations and the tremendous successes that were scored in that war. Never was the life of even a single person risked for our glory. We had the mission of protecting Angola's independence, of defeating the foreign aggression, and every step we took and everything we did was for that purpose.

We were face to face with the South Africans and could have fought some big battles. At one time, we had all the possibilities for inflicting a crushing defeat on them in the military sphere, but that might have cost a number of lives. Whenever we could, we created the balance of power required to determine the outcome of the situation — this happened many times — but, if we could determine that outcome by simply creating the right balance of power and giving our adversary a chance to understand their disadvantageous position and the need to withdraw, we preferred that solution to waging a large-scale battle that might cost the lives of hundreds of people and incalculable injuries, because all large military campaigns have a price. I think that human beings should never draw away from the honest goal they seek and let themselves be influenced by history. That's what I've always felt.

Moreover, when you read the history of the peoples and of humanity, remember the things that individuals have done to make an impression on posterity. Many people in ancient times give me the impression that they did many things in search of a place in history — and this is true of men not only in ancient times but also throughout the last 2,000 years, ever since the birth of Christ. I'm thinking of many leaders and politicians who engaged in great actions, great undertakings, yet you get the impression that they did so in search of personal prominence and even a role in history.

Others tried to perpetuate themselves by means of monuments. For example, what were the huge monuments in Egypt for — the pyramids and temples? Every pharaoh built a big pyramid or temple or house or residence to make his mark and be remembered by posterity. I've often wondered what those great pharaohs — some of them were great warriors, great political figures, great statesmen — would think if they knew that, when their mummies were found, they would wind up in a museum — and not an Egyptian museum, but a museum in New York, London or Paris. I feel rather sad when I think of all that those men did and the tens of thousands of slaves who died while building those things to perpetuate the image or figure of someone and then, after all these years, all that is left is the bitter knowledge that those remains — the remains that were preserved for all eternity — have wound up somewhere else.

If you study the history of humanity, you see that all civilizations in all continents constructed large monuments and other big things to perpetuate something, yet now all that remains is the memory of the architecture, of the feats of the engineers who built those things and the materials with which they did the job. Nobody remembers — or even knows, in many cases — who ordered it done.

If you've had an opportunity to come in close contact with history and analyze these matters, you realize that humans tend to make a fool of themselves if they think too much about posterity and the impression they will make on it. I would say it would be wiser to aspire to a modest, simple, even anonymous place in history, because, if you have a true measure of the power of people as individuals, you know it's so fragile and such a small thing that it really doesn't make sense to magnify the role of any individual, no matter how intelligent, brilliant or able they may be. There have been many able, intelligent, meritorious figures in the course of history.

Tomás Borge: There's a lot of talk about the role of the masses in history...

Fidel Castro: I also observe and learn something else from the people every day: I see so many brilliant, able, meritorious people, so I'm aware of that merit, of the role they have played in all this history and throughout this process. If you're fair, you realize that history is usually unfair to ordinary men and women, attributing too much importance to outstanding figures, to leaders and chiefs. It gives them too much merit and practically ignores the millions, hundreds of thousands, tens of thousands or simply thousands of men and women who made possible the thing that exalted one person over the others, making them important in national and world public opinion. I even think that a strict sense of justice keeps us from toying with the idea of occupying prominent, outstanding places.

I've tried to explain how I view this problem, why I haven't been concerned with it. However, I am very concerned with ideas and the importance of preserving the results of work — that's what is important. If their work should be lost, what would the people who did that work and were trying to reach those goals matter? Anybody who thinks this way, Tomás, can't have paid much attention or given much time to thinking about how much glory they will have or what place they will have in history. I would a thousand times rather think of the place history will assign to the causes and ideas we're defending, to the rights of humanity and to people's happiness in the world of the future.

One of the reasons why I supported José Martí's ideas is expressed in one of the most beautiful things I've ever read of Martí's — as I've read many beautiful things that he wrote, and many of his thoughts have brought me infinite pleasure. It goes like this: All the glory in the world fits in a kernel of corn. What a penetrating thought! How unassuming! What modesty! That's what Martí had. You will never catch him talking about what mark he will make on history or his historical image. He was always dedicated to the work and thinking of the revolution.

Lastly, you have to remember that, in the end, even the light of the stars will be extinguished. The sun will stop shining, and life on Earth will cease to exist — and, at the rate we're going, it seems that, one way or another, there won't be any possibilities for living on Earth within a relatively short period of time. Humans will disappear from this planet called Earth, and I don't think the possibilities are great for moving to the moon, Mars or any other place, because what little is known of the geological, climatic and other natural conditions there shows that it would be impossible. The stars are drawing farther and farther apart, and I can't conceive of even a remote possibility that humans will move to another star.

We know that stars, like human beings, are born, live and die. When the light of our sun is extinguished, that will be the end of history, too. Let's suppose that humans continue to exist up to or nearly up to that moment. Then, what is history? Something that is born — and this is so even of true history, objective history — lives and dies and will never have any witnesses other than humans themselves.

The nearest star is four light-years away and receding in space. If you analyze the laws of physics at all, you don't have to be a pessimist to see that insurmountable barriers prevent humans from moving to another star.

I am sure that other forms of life — even very developed forms of intelligent life — have existed and do exist. Mathematics practically shows that, what with millions of galaxies and infinite millions of stars, phenomena more or less similar to those that gave rise to life on our planet must have arisen elsewhere, too. I don't think that anybody who considers this possibility calmly can deny it. However, everything we know — and we do know something, because modern humans know something of the laws of physics — makes it very difficult to believe in the possibility that intelligent beings from other planets will come to analyze what happened here. So, there won't be any witnesses, and, someday, everything will disappear — even history.

Therefore, we should be unassuming and limit ourselves to doing our duty to the best of our extremely limited possibilities. That's how I understand my role in life, as a revolutionary.

Forgive me for having talked at such length on this topic, but you asked for it, and I wanted to tell you a little of what I thought.

CHAPTER 2

The new world order and the assassination of the Soviet Union

Cuba made exceptional efforts to support the guerrilla struggle that had suddenly appeared like a natural harvest of red roses in many Latin American countries. As for myself, I received help from Ernesto Che Guevara and took part in a frustrated attempt to land weapons for Nicaragua on the northern coast of Honduras.

Many guerrilla groups engaged in armed struggle in Venezuela, Brazil, Colombia, Argentina, Peru and other countries. The most spectacular attempt was that of Bolivia. Nicaragua was something else.

The people's insurrection that toppled the Somoza dictatorship had a natural strength that was so overwhelming that, when we Sandinistas approached Omar Torrijos, Carlos Andrés Pérez, José López Portillo, Rodrigo Carazo and other heads of state and political leaders from all over the world, they unanimously expressed solidarity with Nicaragua and the FSLN.

Thus, when the idea arose of taking weapons to Nicaragua's southern border, Carlos Andrés asked Fidel for help. The weapons arrived at San José's Juan Santamaría Airport and got the green light to be carried along Costa Rican highways.

Fidel, Manuel Piñeiro ("Redbeard") and the top-ranking Sandinista leaders were at the solemn, emotional ceremony held in Havana in February 1979 in which the FSLN achieved internal unity.

On that occasion, the Joint National Leadership of the Sandinista Front was established, consisting of three commanders from each of the sections into which the political-military organization created by Carlos Fonseca had split. The Sandinista leaders promoted that meeting, which Fidel welcomed with respect and joy.

Throughout these years, Fidel always abstained from giving us advice, and his opinions — which he gave only when we asked for them insistently — didn't always coincide with those of the majority of the Sandinista leaders.

He was always sensitive and respectful of our decisions. His only persistent, almost obsessive, recommendation was that we should maintain the internal unity of the FSLN. The Cuban revolutionary leadership and the FSLN have maintained cordial relations, though some contradictions have arisen in Nicaragua's new political conditions.

The FSLN's electoral defeat — heartrending for many and educational for others — came at a time of ideological chill, with the breaking up of the Soviet Union as a geographic unit and the destruction of socialism there.

T. B.

Tomás Borge: It may be said that Cuba is a kind of thus-far-impregnable rock of revolutionary practices and ideas. Unquestionably, socialism collapsed in the Soviet Union and other Eastern European countries, but, just as unquestionably, it has survived in Cuba. Montesquieu said that history is the noise surrounding certain events, but these are facts rather than merely noises, peaks in history that cannot be questioned. Does all this mean, Fidel, that it has become a part of history?

Fidel Castro: I agree with you, Tomás, that the survival of the Cuban Revolution thus far constitutes an outstanding achievement.

You point to our decision to continue advancing when the socialist camp has collapsed and we are the only remaining enemy that imperialism is attacking with fury. Cuba isn't the only socialist country, for we mustn't forget that Korea is a socialist country, China is a socialist country, and Vietnam is a socialist country with tremendous merit. Cuba isn't the only socialist country, but it is the main target, the center, of imperialism's threats and aggressive campaigns — we Cubans and the Cuban Revolution are the main target against which imperialism is directing its guns, and it is employing all of its resources to attack and destroy us. The fact that, after the collapse of the socialist camp and the disappearance of the Soviet Union, Cuba has decided to continue advancing, to confront all those dangers and to take up the challenge, may be considered an outstanding achievement in history when events and the values that certain events embody are viewed objectively.

This is an unusual thing, and it isn't entirely dependent on what we have done thus far. Rather, it also depends on what we're going to do in the future, on our standing firm, on how well we defend the Revolution and our country's sovereignty and independence — on how much we're ready to do to achieve this. This still lies in the future, and it will ultimately determine the importance of what we're doing now.

What we've done is very important — I hope we'll remain true to what we've done thus far, as I think we will when faced with risks of any kind. That will also largely determine the final image of what we're doing now.

This evening, you saw how many Latin Americans came up expressing hope as if telling us, "Stand firm and fight." Many people sent messages exhorting us to fight and stand firm. How well we can stand firm and fight is yet to be seen, but I'm confident that we'll be able do so.

Tomás Borge: You unquestionably have a lot of confidence in that, and I share your confidence. Does this mean that the Cuban Revolution is the beginning of the resurrection of a socialist option at the world level?

Fidel Castro: I think that we're defending certain principles that are of tremendous value at a time of confusion and opportunism in the world, a time when many politicians are feathering their own nests, a time of what you might call the deification of imperialism's military and political power.

Never before has humanity witnessed such an upsurge in the power of reaction and the empire. This doesn't mean that it will be eternal — far from it, for the empire is beset by all kinds of contradictions. But this is the time we're in, and I think that, right now, the preservation of values is of decisive importance for all progressives, all true democrats and all revolutionaries — all who want the best for humanity and who cherish the noblest sentiments. Preserving those values is of unquestionable importance.

No matter what happens, other times will come. Right now, we're in the midst of a huge reactionary wave; later, a huge revolutionary wave, a huge progressive wave, will come again. That is for certain. This is the reactionary high water mark; with or without us, another progressive, revolutionary wave will sweep the world. When I say "revolutionary," I'm referring to goals and purposes, not to the form in which those ideas are propagated. Just as reactionary ideas now prevail and are very strong, the time will come when progressive, democratic, fair ideas will prevail — whether or not we are here.

I think — I've always thought this — that flags and other symbols have great value. Therefore, even though we are a solitary islet, the very fact that we exist at all is of great value. If we defend this solitary islet to the death, that will be of great value, too. If our enemies invade us and we stand firm, come what may, that will be of great value. If we win, as we unquestionably would, because it would be impossible to exterminate millions of men and women who are determined to fight to the death, that would be of great value for the ideas, the principles and the cause that we are defending. Nobody can take that away from us — that's in our own hands, no one elses.

Therefore, I think that what we're doing is of great importance for the future, but it doesn't make us believe that the future is entirely dependent on us. It gives us great encouragement to know that we're defending that future and that we're a symbol of that future and of those principles for a world filled with people who are hungry, exploited and suffering.

We have a clear, precise idea of our role, and all of those factors stimulate and encourage us in the struggle. That is the link between what we're doing and what we're ready to do, on the one hand, and the future, on the other. I think it will always be of great value.

Tomás Borge: Not long ago, referring not to socialism in general but to the specific case of the Soviet Union, you said it had been stabbed in the back. Was Mikhail Gorbachev one of the assassins involved in the white dagger plot against the Soviet Union?

Fidel Castro: No, I wouldn't describe Gorbachev that way. I don't look on him as an assassin who engaged in the premeditated destruction of the Soviet Union.

The Soviet Union is an incredible case of self-destruction. Unquestionably, the leaders, the ones who governed that country, were responsible for that self-destruction. Some destroyed it wittingly; others, unwittingly. That, more or less, is what I meant to say: that everything they did led to the destruction of the Soviet Union; all of the phenomena and all of the tendencies that were unleashed there led to destruction. We saw this right from the beginning — or soon after the beginning — when a series of phenomena of that kind began to appear.

I can't say that Gorbachev acted wittingly in the destruction of the Soviet Union, because I'm sure that he intended to struggle to improve socialism; I have no doubts about that. I conversed with him several times, and I got to know him a little. He was very friendly, a friend, to us. For a long time, as long as he had real power in the Soviet Union, he did everything possible to respect Cuba's interests and to preserve the good relations between the Soviet Union and our country. Nevertheless, he unquestionably played an important role in the events that took place in the Soviet Union.

Tomás Borge: Have you read Gorbachev's book *Perestroika*?

Fidel Castro: I read Gorbachev's book, which was sold all over the world, with close attention, trying to understand his aims. Often, I felt that he was doing things too quickly, that he wanted to solve many problems all at once. They had to have established priorities in the process for improving socialism in the Soviet Union. I am sure that it was a very desirable and useful thing to improve socialism in the Soviet Union — not put an end to socialism in the Soviet Union or destroy that powerful state. The Soviet Union played an extremely important role in the world balance of power and was of key importance for all of the Third World countries and for everybody, because it was the only power that could — and did — confront the power of U.S. imperialism.

So, whatever mistakes the Soviets may have made and whatever deficiencies Soviet socialism may have had, the objective role it played in the world was of transcendental importance, and it should have been preserved, no matter what.

Tomás Borge: It's one thing to preserve socialism, Fidel, and another to preserve the Soviet Union...

Fidel Castro: We thought that the efforts the Soviets were making to improve socialism in the Soviet Union were good, but we couldn't be in agreement, nor would we ever have been in agreement, with the destruction of the Soviet Union — with the destruction not only of socialism in the Soviet Union but also of the Soviet Union itself — because of the terrible damage that would do to all of the peoples of the world and because of the situation in which it would place the Third World, in particular. It even created a difficult situation for the allies of the United States and inaugurated a new period in history with the collapse not only of the socialist camp but of the Soviet Union, as well. Everything was swept away in the very short time of just a few years.

I was telling you that, when I read Gorbachev's book, I saw that he didn't want that. Gorbachev spoke of defending socialism and of having more — not less — socialism. He repeated that many times, and I don't doubt that that's what he wanted. But a process was unleashed for which Gorbachev and the other Soviet leaders, the leadership of the Soviet Party and government as a whole, were responsible. I'm not talking about individual responsibility here; they should be held collectively responsible for what happened. They made enormous mistakes and unleashed a process that was self-destructive for socialism and for the Soviet Union. If you start a process in which all of a country's values begin to be destroyed, that process is very negative.

A process was unleashed that destroyed the authority of the Party, which meant destroying one of the pillars of socialism and of the Soviet Union, because the Party which Lenin founded was the main pillar in the creation of the Soviet Union. The creation of that Party was an unprecedented historic feat and a tremendous achievement of the Soviet peoples.

If you destroy the authority of the state, the consequences are terrible. I don't think Gorbachev intended to destroy those values, the Party or the state, but that was the final result of the process that began with perestroika, which sought to overcome the deficiencies of socialism, improve socialism and consolidate the values of socialism and the history of that country.

Tomás Borge: A short while ago, we spoke about history... Will this negative process change what has been known as the history of the Soviet Union?

Fidel Castro: One of the negative processes that was unleashed was the destruction of the history of the Soviet Union. It's a matter not of the analysis or criticism of problems, but of the destruction and negation of all of the values, merits and history of the Soviet Union. Nobody there envisaged or could conceive of such a thing. I can't believe that Gorbachev and many of the other men who initiated that process had that intention. They did make enormous mistakes by failing to foresee the consequences of what they were doing and by not doing the right thing to reach the goals and purposes they proclaimed — which, of course, were necessary and legitimate.

At one point in his book, Gorbachev says, more or less, "Some people think you have to tackle problems progressively. No, the correct thing is to tackle them all at once, to do it all at the same time."

Many of the strategic and tactical mistakes that were made were viewed as the correct way of doing things. Then, when all of those negative tendencies were unleashed, opportunistic elements were also introduced, plus all of the elements that wittingly acted to destroy socialism. Naturally, the United States and its Western allies helped to destroy socialism in the Soviet Union, urging on the reactionary forces there. People in the West even changed the terminology, describing those who wanted to defend the Soviet Union, socialism and communism as "conservatives," and those who wanted capitalism — not modern capitalism, but primitive capitalism, which is what is being applied there right now — neoliberalism and even the disappearance of the Soviet Union as "progressives" and "leftists." All of the concepts were deliberately twisted.

Western propaganda promoted that process, because it wanted to force the Soviet Union to its knees. The imperialists did so much that, now, they're worried by what has happened and by the possible consequences of that disintegration.

Tomás Borge: Do you believe that through some turn of events it would have been possible to save the territorial integrity of the Soviet Union?

Fidel Castro: Imperialism couldn't have destroyed the Soviet Union if the Soviets themselves hadn't destroyed it first, if those responsible for strategy and tactics and the members of the political leadership and government of the country hadn't already destroyed their country, which is what happened. Socialism didn't die a natural death — it was assassinated. That's what I meant.

We don't yet know exactly what happened. People are beginning to say — and I don't want to get into this subject — that the changes in Poland were carefully planned and drawn up by the West and that the whole process of disintegration of the socialist camp in Eastern Europe was planned and prepared.

Tomás Borge: Do you have any idea, Fidel, of who inside the socialist countries took part in carrying out that plan?

Fidel Castro: The names of those who worked wittingly with the CIA, who worked with the U.S. intelligence services as a fifth column to destroy the socialist camp, aren't known yet but will be known someday, as will the names of those who worked wittingly in complicity with the intelligence services of the United States to destroy socialism in the Soviet Union and to destroy the Soviet Union itself. They will be known someday; that information always comes out. It may take 20, 25, 40 or 50 years, but someday they will be known.

This doesn't mean that history ended there. Right now, there is so much uncertainty and such a difficult process of conflicts, problems and splits that it's painful to see. It makes you bitter to think that the phenomenon of disintegration that took place there may not yet have reached its depths. I really don't know how those nations are going to survive if they destroy the economic ties that still bind them. You can't set up a shared economy in 70 years and then have all of it suddenly disintegrate. We don't know how much suffering, how many calamities and how much it may cost for each of the peoples that used to form part of the Soviet Union.

Since the Soviet Union disappeared, the least you can hope for is that those countries maintain some kind of economic integration and cooperation, a coordinated defense system and the same boundaries as the republics that withdrew from the Soviet Union, and that new processes of disintegration won't take place within them. Everything that may take place in terms of more division, conflicts and disintegration among the countries that used to constitute the Soviet Union will be very bad for all humanity and will facilitate conditions propitious for the United States' world hegemony, world domination, and exploitation by imperialism and its current allies. In the new conditions, we have yet to see where the contradictions that will arise between the United States and its allies will lead.

This is a law of history. There are no exceptions, and it is inexorable: more and more contradictions will arise among those who are now allies. With the disappearance of the Soviet Union, absolutely new conditions are being created in the world and rivalries are beginning to emerge between the major capitalist economic powers. Another history is beginning. We don't know how that process in the Soviet Union will end, what things may happen if the problems those people have aren't solved or what even worse consequences that process may have for these people and for all humanity.

Now they'll have the experience of capitalism — the worst form of capitalism — and of neoliberalism. They'll experience the International Monetary Fund formula. They'll share the experiences of the Latin American peoples and those of Africa and Asia — the experiences of the Third World. This is a history that is just beginning, in which nobody has had the last word. This phenomenon is advancing, as are many other negative trends. Eventually, they'll stop gaining ground, and then they should begin to be reversed, until everything that can be salvaged from what used to be the old community of countries that formed the Soviet Union is saved.

Tomás Borge: Unquestionably, the United States and its allies are, or were, overjoyed by what happened there. A European head of state told me in confidence that he felt very nostalgic about the Soviet Union, which confirms what you've just said.

In the late 1980s, we saw more effective participation by international agencies in the search for justice. Why was that tendency frustrated? In your opinion, can it be reactivated?

Fidel Castro: I think that the events we've been talking about had a lot to do with this new trend. When you speak of the international agencies, I think you're mainly referring to those of the United Nations.

It's true that there was a positive trend in the United Nations more than 10 years ago. It approved the Charter of Economic Rights and Duties of States and the New International Economic Order. United Nations institutions have worked in various fields to try to solve humanity's problems — they've made efforts on behalf of children, women, development, education, public health, the environment, culture and many other things. I think that the United Nations agencies in general have played a positive role, but as soon as the United Nations — and especially the Security Council — began to turn into a tool of U.S. hegemony, then, logically, a situation was created that is of concern to the world.

Many things have contributed to this: not only the collapse of the socialist camp and the disintegration of the Soviet Union, but also the Persian Gulf War and the mistakes that some Third World countries made. I think that Iraq made some serious mistakes that gave the United States a golden opportunity for making its debut as the master of the world, waging a technological war there, establishing itself in the Middle East, increasing its role as gendarme and facilitating its maneuvers for controlling the Security Council.

All of those factors have contributed to the present situation. Those events helped imperialism to monopolize everything for its own benefit and helped to create this critical situation and the reversal of the positive role that the United Nations had been playing, in spite of its limitations. It has an undemocratic structure, because the permanent members of the Security Council have the right to veto — a right the United States has exercised I don't know how many dozens of times. I don't know the exact figure, but it hasn't hesitated to exercise that right on countless occasions when it deemed a veto beneficial to its national interests and those of its closest allies.

In spite of that, I agree that there was a positive trend in the role the international agencies were playing; it has been reversed, just like the world situation.

Tomás Borge: In the present conditions, what new contradictions can you see? Specifically, what form will the North-South contradiction take?

Fidel Castro: Tomás, you're asking a lot of questions that I must mull over. I don't think about these things all the time, and I don't have a lot of time for theorizing about or delving into all those problems, especially in a situation in which I have a tremendous load of practical work, intensive work every day to meet my obligations, but I'm going to try to answer some of those questions without going into detail.

In the current world situation, the first and main contradiction will be the one between the interests of the Third World countries and those of the developed capitalist countries. There will be two contradictions which are partly the same, yet different: the contradiction between the interests of the Third World countries and those of the developed capitalist countries, and the contradiction between the interests of the Third World countries — and the world in general — and the hegemonistic interests of the United States.

I think that other important contradictions will arise between the big capitalist economic powers: between the interests of the

United States, those of Japan and the rest of Southeast Asia and those of the European Community. These will be sharp contradictions that will inevitably develop in the new conditions. Right now, the countries of the former Soviet Union and the formerly socialist European countries have, in fact, joined the Third World countries in competing for the few financial resources in the world.

Moreover, the West is trying to incorporate into its orbit the formerly socialist European countries and the countries that used to constitute the Soviet Union, having them participate in unequal terms of trade and the privileges characteristic of that trade between industrialized countries and the Third World. At one time the trade between those socialist countries, which had some level of development, and the Third World countries wasn't governed by the same principles of trade that the developed capitalist countries imposed on the world. Now all of those countries that have some level of development will try to join — and the West will try to have them join — the international economic order established by imperialism and to benefit from unequal terms of trade with the Third World countries while, at the same time, competing with those countries for the few financial resources now available. Many people need money now: the United States, which will have a budgetary deficit of $400 billion this year (an all-time record); the Third World; and the formerly socialist countries and the countries that used to constitute the Soviet Union, which are already asking for a lot of money.

Those, I think, are the main contradictions that can be seen in the immediate future. They are already beginning to be expressed in various ways and will become more and more acute in the near future, in the short and medium terms.

CHAPTER 3

Stalin

Like many revolutionaries of my time, I was a Stalinist at one point. Ever since adolescence, I considered that defiant moustache venerable. I thought that everything that was said against the Soviet leader — frequently in an exaggerated way — was obscene calumny.

I had read what Lenin had said in December 1922 and January 1923 — "Comrade Stalin... has unlimited authority concentrated in his hands, and I am not sure whether he will always be capable of using that authority with sufficient caution"; and "Stalin is too rude" and that it was necessary, to seek "another man... [who is] more tolerant, more loyal, more polite and more considerate to the comrades, less capricious" — but those assessments seemed to me to be too subjective.

Long before the Nicaraguan Revolution triumphed, my idol was proved to have feet of clay. Gradually, I grew more aware of that shadow of horror that followed the enlightened birth of the October Revolution.

From his political exile in Paris, Régis Debray declared some weeks ago that Fidel Castro was "Trotsky, Lenin and Stalin, all wrapped up in one caudillo."

Even though Fidel has the intellectual quality of Trotsky, the integrity of Lenin and the organizational ability of Stalin, it is impossible to compare him with those historic figures. To do so would be equivalent to continuing to use European values and processes as obligatory models, and we Latin Americans are tired of doing that.

Fidel is Fidel. He is a "caudillo" only in the sense that Túpac Amaru, Bolívar, San Martín, Hidalgo, Martí, Morazán and Sandino were, in times of glory for Our America.

In Cuba, any cult that may exist is fully justified by Fidel's personality. Fidel is unquestionably an archetype.

What he says here may help us to have a more objective view of an important figure in the revolutionary movement who has always been surrounded by controversy.

T. B.

Tomás Borge: Most of the Latin American revolutionary leaders believe that Joseph Stalin was the mastermind behind the present crisis of socialism. What do you think?

Fidel Castro: You can't — or, at least, I wouldn't — say that. I think that Stalin made some very serious mistakes, but he also had some very great successes. Stalin played an important role in the October Revolution and in the war against foreign intervention after the Revolution; all that is history. Stalin played an important role in the industrialization of the Soviet Union and in the Great Patriotic War and the reconstruction of the country. Those are facts.

Tomás Borge: Some people say the Soviet Union won the war in spite of Stalin...

Fidel Castro: Tomás, for many years I've felt critical of what Stalin did in many fields, which makes me think I have some basis for being objective in all this. It seems to me that it would be very superficial historically to blame Stalin for the things that have occurred in the Soviet Union, because no one man, by himself, could create certain conditions. It would be just as wrong as to credit Stalin for the achievements of the Soviet Union — impossible! I think it was the efforts of millions of heroic people that made it possible for the Soviet Union to be created, develop, become a reality and play a very important role in the world, benefiting hundreds of millions of people.

I think that, if we have to think in terms of individuals, Lenin should be given the main credit for the October Revolution. Lenin had tremendous, singular, outstanding merit far above that of all the other leaders. We should keep in mind, first of all, that the Soviet Union had the misfortune of Lenin dying relatively young

— it needed him to live a further 10, 15 or 20 years.

Those of us who have studied Lenin, all of us who know of his thinking and his enormous talent, are aware that Lenin would have been able to rectify many of the negative trends that arose within the Soviet revolutionary process after his death. Thus, Lenin's absence — the vacuum his death left in the theoretical sphereas well as in the construction of socialism in the Soviet Union — is a factor that had a great influence on what happened later.

I was telling you that I've been critical of Stalin in many regards — first of all, for his infringements of legality. Stalin committed enormous abuses of power.

Speaking in general terms of what I consider the worst mistakes Stalin made, I would say that, in his agricultural policy, for a long time he placed his trust in small farms and private ownership; he didn't develop a progressive process of socialization of the land. For some years, a situation was maintained in which all food production was dependent on individual plots, until, at one point, those plots had given all that they could, and food production was completely paralyzed. I think that the process of socialization of the land should have been started earlier and developed progressively. It seems to me that the attempt to socialize the land in an extremely short period of time historically, by means of violence, was very costly, both economically and in terms of human suffering. That was a serious mistake made under Stalin's leadership.

In this regard, I can tell you about our own experience — we reason with facts, not arguments. First of all, we didn't have the kind of agrarian reform that the other socialist countries had. We gave ownership of the land to all of the sharecroppers, tenant farmers, squatters and others who worked the land, but we didn't divide up the large landholdings; we didn't break them up. If we had done that, we would have destroyed our country's sugar industry — it would have been terrible, and that industry would almost entirely have disappeared. We would have destroyed our possibilities for feeding the people if we had created hundreds of thousands of new small farms in our country.

Of course, it's very easy to pass judgment in different

conditions. The Soviets may not have had any alternative to dividing it all up. At the time in which they were living, their poverty and lack of resources, the blockade and all the other problems they had may have made it impossible for them to have had any other kind of agrarian reform. I admit that necessity may have forced them to act the way they did. What I don't believe is that anything forced them to have then carried out an accelerated process of compulsory collectivization. We didn't split up large estates into smaller plots. We gave title to everybody who was working a bit of land, but we also created state ownership as the basis for large-scale agricultural production. No other country in the world as small as Cuba exports as much food as we do per capita. Each year, we export enough food for 40 million people, and we have been doing this for the last 15 years, even though our population has been growing and we've had less and less land to work with, because we've been building installations of all kinds. If we had divided the land up into small plots, we wouldn't have been able to do this.

This is something that isn't widely known: how much food, per capita, does Cuba export? For every citizen, we have been exporting enough food for four people, and we've been able to do this because we didn't have that kind of agrarian reform; we knew enough to avoid that pitfall.

Secondly, we gave title to the farmers who already owned land but didn't have the papers to prove it. We've always understood that small plots of land have limited production possibilities, but we never engaged in any kind of compulsory collectivization. We promoted a slow, gradual collectivization process among the small farmers — who have played an important role in Cuba's agricultural production and own a considerable proportion of the land — and, in a little over 10 years, around 50 percent of the small owners were to pool their land. The other 50 percent held on to their holdings, and we have respected that. We work with them and carry out our food program in conjunction with them, no matter what the technical limitations of a small plot may be. For example, you can't use central pivot irrigation equipment that irrigates 100 hectares on such small plots; it would be impossible. You can't use planes or cane harvesters or the latest, highest-productivity techniques. Even so, it never even occurred to us to force the 50 percent of the independent owners who remained after the cooperatives were developed to join in socialized agriculture. We've given them guarantees and security, and we have promised them that, if they want to stay there all their lives, they may do so. We will always respect their decision. We carried out the process of collectivization among the independent farmers who owned their own land — land that we had given them — on the basis of strict respect for their wishes.

You can imagine the consequences that the process of compulsory collectivization must have had for a country in which the vast majority of the people were farmers and where the land had been parcelled out at first — perhaps as a basic political and social necessity, perhaps because nothing else could have been done at that time. That, in my opinion, was one of Stalin's biggest mistakes.

Tomás Borge: Going back to the topic of military leadership in World War II, what do you think of Stalin's role?
Fidel Castro: I think that Stalin's policy on the eve of the war was totally erroneous.

You can understand Stalin's motivations in his international policy. I think it is an historically proved fact that he wanted to set up a coalition against Hitler. Why? There are documents and proof of all kinds showing that the Western powers, the capitalist countries, wanted to pit Hitler against the Soviet Union. History clearly shows that the German bourgeoisie looked with approval and even in a kindly way on Hitler and that it supported Nazism as a tool against Communism. Even though Hitler was — and showed that he was — a fanatical racist, that was forgiven because he presented himself as a champion of the struggle against Communism, and everybody viewed Hitler as the instrument for destroying the Soviet Union.

I was 13 when World War II began, and I read all the newspapers. I had been avidly reading all of the newspapers, all the international news, ever since the Spanish Civil War. The Civil War was in 1936, when I was nearly 10, and I still remember, as clearly as if I had just read it, a lot of the news that came in. A lot of Spaniards lived on my father's farm, and some of them didn't know how to read and write. Some of them were Republicans — many of those Spaniards were Republicans by instinct — and some supported Franco. Anyway, they used to ask me to read the newspaper to them. For example, I read the news to the cook in our house. He was a Galician of peasant origin, illiterate and a staunch Republican — it seems that rebelliousness against feudalism and exploitation ran in his blood. I remember all of the battles in Asturias and Teruel and on the Ebro; I kept close tabs on all that.

I read the newspapers in the years preceding World War II, and I read the news every day during the war years. This is without mentioning the books I read about the military events of the time and about political events after the war.

I've been reading about those things for 50 years, and, as I told you, I was 13 when it all began. I've remembered many things and made political and even military analyses of all that.

Nobody can deny that the Western powers encouraged Hitler until he became a monster, a real menace. Nor can anybody deny the extraordinary weakness with which the Western powers dealt with Hitler and their conduct in the days leading up to his annexation of Austria — the famous Anschluss — first of all, with the occupation of the Saar, where he had been told he mustn't send troops, and even up to Hitler and Mussolini's intervention in Spain.

It was German pilots and bombers that destroyed Guernica and bombed Madrid, killing hundreds of thousands of Spaniards. German and Italian planes, as part of an unmistakably expansionist policy, among other factors, determined the outcome of the war. No English, French or U.S. planes fought on the side of the Spanish Republic, though brigades of international volunteers did. The only country that really helped Spain was the Soviet Union.

You can't deny the historical fact that most of the weapons with which the Spanish Republicans fought came from the Soviet Union, as did the few planes the Republic had and its tanks and artillery. The Soviets gave what they could and sent it there.

What other country did that when Hitler and Mussolini began to carry out their expansionist policy? And, in the end, Hitler and Mussolini achieved their goal of wiping the Spanish Republic off the face of the earth. What did the West do? What did the Western powers do? In the midst of those events, Germany rearmed. What did the West do to prevent German rearmament?

Then came the occupation of all those areas of European territory where Hitler's army had no right to go. Later on, the Germans annexed Austria and expanded. Then came Munich, and they grabbed a part of Czechoslovakia; soon afterwards, they occupied the rest of the country. German influence and expansion advanced toward Hungary, Romania and Bulgaria, sending troops all over.

What did the West do in view of all those movements? It left the Soviet Union to stand alone. The Soviet Union was very frightened by that maneuver — it saw that everyone tolerated Hitler's penetration in the Danube and strategic areas. Naturally, that acquiesence stimulated Hitler's expansionism and Stalin's fear, which led Stalin to do something that I will always criticize, because I think it was really a flagrant violation of principle: his seeking peace with Hitler at all costs, to gain time.

In our long revolutionary life and in the already relatively long history of the Cuban Revolution, we have never negotiated even one principle to gain time or to obtain any other kind of practical advantage. I think that his doing so was a terrible mistake. I'm not going to say he was the only one to blame, because I think the policies of the Western countries forced him into that position. But he entered into the well-known Molotov-Ribbentrop Pact, when the Germans were already beginning to demand that the Danzig Corridor be handed over to them. They made a series of demands concerning Poland, and that is when the pact was signed.

All my life, ever since I developed a political and revolutionary awareness, I have considered that pact to have been a terrible mistake in Soviet foreign policy, a mistake that Stalin made in those years leading up to the war.

Moreover, I think that, far from providing more time, that nonaggression pact reduced the time available. Anyway, the war began. And when Hitler attacked Poland, England and France had no alternative to declaring war.

What consequences did the war have? What followed was Hitler's blitzkrieg, the invasion of Norway, then the occupation of Belgium and Holland, the attack on France, and the defeat of France and England in the Continent. Hitler's power increased throughout Europe and Mussolini entered the war opportunistically, believing that France would collapse. Hitler became more powerful every month, with more and more human and material resources — more fuel, minerals and everything — and became a much more powerful enemy for the Soviet Union.

Then, also in that period, in that situation, Stalin and Hitler began to compete. As Hitler advanced eastward, trying to win positions and seize territory and strategic advantages, it became obvious that war would break out.

What do I think of all that? Do the reasons for some of the Soviets' actions at that time have any weight? Stalin said, "Here's a Russian population, and I want to protect it; I shouldn't let the Germans come; I'll occupy this territory." That's where, in my opinion, he made another big mistake: just when Poland was being attacked, he sent troops to occupy that territory that had been under dispute because it had a Ukrainian population — or Russian, I don't recall which.

What would have been a better policy? I'm sure that, if we had found ourselves in a situation such as that, we would have done something else. Rather than give the impression that we were attacking the rear of that country Hitler had invaded, we would have invited the population to cross over to the other side of the border to seek protection, but we wouldn't have trespassed across the border of that country and wouldn't have fought with that country when Hitler was attacking it, no matter what our ideological differences might have been. I think it was a terrible mistake from the point of view of principles and of international opinion.

All my life, I've thought that the little war against Finland was another terrible mistake, both from the viewpoint of principles and from that of international law. That's what I have always thought.

He went on making one mistake after another that brought the Soviet Union into disrepute among large sectors of world public opinion and placed Communists throughout the world — who expressed great solidarity with and were good friends of the Soviet Union — in an extremely difficult position, having to defend all those things in their own countries. Communists all over the world — those were the years of the International — had to engage in a kind of hari-kari to defend the Soviet Union. It was correct to defend the Soviet Union — I'm not saying it wasn't. They couldn't abandon the Soviet Union, no matter what mistakes it made, but they found themselves forced to defend such unpopular things as the Molotov-Ribbentrop Pact, the occupation of a part of Polish territory and the war with Finland.

Now that we're talking about this, I should take the opportunity to tell you that I've never spoken about these things this way with any journalist before.

I think that they were terrible political mistakes — and mistakes of principle, as well — that we would never have made. The history of the Cuban Revolution bears this out, because the Revolution never abandoned its principles. Never, for national convenience or any other reason, did the Revolution abandon any legitimate cause in the world, nor did it abandon any revolutionary movements, even though our adversary was the powerful U.S. government. The history of the Revolution shows that we never abandoned our principles.

The things I mentioned go contrary to principles and doctrine; they even go contrary to political wisdom. Even though it is true that the Soviet Union had a year and nine months between September 1939 and June 1941 in which to rearm, the one who made himself much stronger — 10 times as strong — was Hitler.

Paying an extremely high political and moral price, the Soviet Union managed to increase its military power, but Hitler became 10 times as powerful in the same time.

If Hitler had gone to war against the Soviet Union in 1939, he would have done it less damage than he did in June 1941. Faced not only with the Soviet Army, which had many brave officers who were veterans of the wars of the October Revolution, but also with the always combative and courageous Soviet people, he would have met the same fate as Napoleon Bonaparte. With the people's participation in irregular warfare, the Soviet Union would have defeated Hitler. Therefore, I have always considered the pact to have been a terrible mistake by Stalin and the other Soviet leaders.

Lastly, Stalin's character — his terrible distrust of everything — led him to make other serious mistakes. One of them was to fall into the trap of German intrigue and carry out a huge, terrible, bloody purge of the Armed Forces, in which he practically decapitated the Soviet Army on the eve of the war.

He made another extremely serious mistake in June 1941 when the Germans had concentrated millions of soldiers, thousands of planes, tens of thousands of tanks and armored vehicles and hundreds of divisions — German, Romanian, Hungarian and even Finnish divisions — along the border. Faced with such clearly aggressive intentions — it was impossible to disguise them — Stalin clung to the theory that it was an act of provocation, that everything he had heard and all the information he had received about the concentration was an act of provocation, and acted like an ostrich, sticking his head in the sand. He didn't mobilize the troops. Whenever the leaders of any country see that aggression is imminent, the first thing they do is declare a general mobilization. But the Soviet Union, that could have mobilized many millions of people — farmers, soldiers and workers — and all the population and that had thousands of planes and thousands of tanks, didn't mobilize them even gradually or decree an immediate general mobilization. Instead, it adopted what I consider to have been an absurd, excessively cautious position, so as not to give Hitler any pretext for moving against it. That's why it didn't mobilize the Army and didn't declare any general mobilization.

So, what happened? After all of the Soviet Union's mistakes — that was in 1941 — Hitler launched a surprise attack on the Soviet Union on June 22. I think it was on a weekend, a Saturday or Sunday.

How can you launch a "surprise" attack with millions of soldiers? Well, it was done, and Hitler's troops attacked a country that wasn't mobilized. The officers and many of the soldiers, including those stationed in the air units and airfields on the front line, had been given passes on the day of the attack.

It was always very, very clear to me what they should have done at that moment: declare a general mobilization and move the planes and such things far back. If they weren't going to attack, if they adopted a defensive policy, they should have moved all of their planes far back, mobilized all their reserves, concentrated those reserves at strategic points and had all of its forces on the front line in a state of maximum alert. Then Hitler wouldn't have been able to launch a surprise attack and inflict such heavy initial losses on them.

When Yugoslavia was invaded — which may have delayed Hitler's attack on the Soviet Union by some weeks — the Soviet Union should already have been mobilized. If it had done that in 1941, I am absolutely sure that Hitler's army would have been smashed to smithereens by the Soviet Army deep in Soviet territory, and it wouldn't have surrounded millions of soldiers, taken hundreds of thousands of prisoners in the first few weeks of the war, destroyed almost all of the Soviet planes on the first day and caused the enormous destruction it did in the first few weeks and months of the war. It wouldn't have reached Moscow, Kiev, Stalingrad or any of those places. That would have been impossible, because that immense country would have swallowed the German armies if its people had been mobilized. I think that world history would even have been different, and, if the Soviet Union had done what it should have done on the eve of the German aggression, World War II would have ended not in Berlin but in Portugal if Hitler's troops hadn't surrendered.

Tomás Borge: The Soviets would have occupied all of Europe, or at least through France...

Fidel Castro: Naturally, if they defeated Hitler in Berlin or on Germany's western border, they wouldn't have had to keep on advancing, but Hitler's troops occupied France — though not Spain, which had a friendly government. So, if the fighting had continued up to the end, the war would have ended in Portugal. There wouldn't even have been a Second Front, and the U.S. troops wouldn't have landed in Europe. I'm absolutely convinced of this, and I've always been sure of it, ever since I analyzed all of those events.

So, I've listed Stalin's worst mistakes, including abuses of power, violations of the law, and the acts of cruelty that he did, in fact, commit. In my view, they were basic mistakes.

Tomás Borge: What, in your opinion, did Stalin do that was to his credit?

Fidel Castro: Without going into detail, he deserves credit for having unified the Soviet Union, consolidating the work Lenin had begun in terms of the unity of the Party and giving impetus to the international revolutionary movement. That is unquestionable. The industrialization of the Soviet Union was a great success — it took great effort and was greatly to Stalin's credit, and I think it was of decisive importance in the Soviet Union's ability to stand firm.

Another of Stalin's great successes was the program for moving the war industry and the basic strategic industries to Siberia and deep into other parts of the Soviet Union. Rather, it is to the credit of his group, but people are now blaming him as an individual and giving him individual credit for the successes that were scored, even though they were really successes and mistakes of many people.

I think that, once the war had begun, he did a good job of leading the Soviet Union. He had some initial moments of great confusion — that has been historically proved, and Mikoyan told me about Stalin's first hours. He was very bitter, as all of his assumptions had fallen through. The reports he had received were more than acts of provocation, the Soviet Union had been taken by surprise and Hitler had done it a terrible amount of damage. There were some hours and even some days when he was in great confusion, then he reacted and became a capable military leader. He was the only one who could carry out those functions, for nobody else had the authority, the prestige and the power for playing that role. From then on, he dedicated himself to the defense of the Soviet Union, and many of the generals — Zhukov and other brilliant Soviet generals — said that Stalin played an extremely important role in the defense of the Soviet Union in the war against Nazism. Everybody recognizes that.

The time will come when an impartial analysis is made of him and he isn't blamed for everything that happened, because, when you get right down to it, the Soviet Union we knew was very powerful. Barely four years after atom bombs were dropped on Hiroshima and Nagasaki — actions that gave the United States a monopoly on nuclear weapons — the Soviet Union had nuclear weapons, too. Very shortly afterwards, it also had thermonuclear weapons, and it didn't take long before it also had the means for transporting them. It developed rocketry and space flights and achieved extraordinary levels of development and of industrial and food production.

During some years, the Soviet Union produced more than 200 million tons of foodstuffs. At the time of the outbreak of World War II, the Soviet Union was producing barely 50 or 60 million tons of wheat a year.

I'm not going to go into that now, but the Soviet Union we knew was a very rich country, with enormous economic resources, raw materials, industrial resources and scientific resources. It was a superpower.

Did Stalin have anything to do with the development of that superpower? Of course he did. So, how can people blame Stalin for everything bad that has happened in the Soviet Union? To do so is to take a very superficial view of history, and I won't accept that. It would be like saying that Lenin was to blame because he promoted the socialist revolution, seized the Winter Palace and set up a soviet government — things such as that. How many people could you blame if you were to take that approach? You would end up blaming God because He didn't make Lenin healthy enough to live 15 or 20 years longer.

I don't want to joke about this, though I could say some funny things. The facts show that others inherited that powerful state and destroyed it in just a few years — doing what Hitler and world reaction had tried unsuccessfully to do. They destroyed that powerful country, which had held together even when more than 20 million of its citizens were killed. They bear a great responsibility, which history will assign to them some day, for, with their actions, imperialism achieved its goals without having firing a shot.

We must be objective — analyze all of Stalin's political mistakes, his failures to uphold principles and his successes; delve deeply into the factors that really brought about the destruction of the Soviet Union; and assess the real responsibility of each person. The construction of socialism in the Soviet Union was the first experience of that kind in the history of humanity. No revolutionary process has been without mistakes; no revolution has failed to make big mistakes. Think about the French Revolution, the classical revolutions, the historical revolutions. Think, in Latin America, of the Mexican Revolution, an important historic event that preceded the Bolshevik Revolution — it had violence, illegal actions, a little bit of everything. And what about the French Revolution? And then, with the Restoration, weren't there more illegal actions? Those phenomena have occurred in all revolutions.

At one time, I said we felt proud of having made only a minimum of mistakes and of having avoided many of the mistakes that were made in all of the other revolutions. I could list them, but we aren't talking about that now.

Could anybody conceive of a revolution in the old empire of the Czars without a lot of mistakes? Impossible. So, a revolution took place that had many mistakes and many successes, Tomás, and it played a very important role in the world, because the existence of the Soviet Union and its struggles speeded the revolutionary process in the world. The Soviet Union kept humanity from falling under fascist rule; it speeded the revolutionary process in China, which was an event of singular importance; it contributed to the independence of Vietnam; it helped the liberation movement in Africa and all over the world; and it gave the other peoples a breather in which to live, in a world filled with the antagonisms of two great powers. For all who didn't want to fall under the yoke of U.S. imperialism, the existence of the Soviet Union constituted an enormous advantage, which was lost when the Soviet Union disappeared.

CHAPTER 4

De-ideologization and neoliberalism

If there is anything that is an affront to human intelligence, it is the pretension that ideologies are on the way out.

For some, revolutionary ideas — patched up and on the defensive — have been condemned to extinction, and they talk your ear off about de-ideologization.

This is one of those words that should be thrown out, with the hope that not even a bad poet will include them in one of their works. Without making any great effort, I can imagine de-ideologization as something amorphous, sticky and lacking content, first cousin to brimstone.

Some people want us to de-ideologize everything: economic discussions, political proposals and international relations. That is, they want to ideologize everything in another way. And, to that end, they invite us with supreme courtesy to pay fealty to the new order.

Everything's fine: how beautiful are the women offering themselves in European shopwindows; how picturesque are the children rummaging through the garbage cans of Managua, Lagos and Manila. This is the best of all possible worlds: how elegantly our governments genuflect before the International Monetary Fund; how beautifully exploited are nations and men and women.

They shout, "Don't lift a finger against the system or cast aspersions on capitalism, or God will punish you."

We already know that de-ideologization isn't the end of ideologies; rather, it is the illegible sign of the attempted burial of Marxism hidden away in the political crypts of Europe and, it would seem, in the ballot boxes of Nicaragua.

According to this argument, the Cubans did wrong when they nationalized all the businesses and established a state monopoly on banking and foreign trade. They profaned the principles of free enterprise and free trade, abused immaculate private property and stuck the state's nose into economic life. They also got their hands dirty when they promoted education that had an objective view of nature and society and didn't respect the Holy Inquisition and half a dozen papal encyclicals.

In speaking on this topic, Fidel Castro brings out the cunning ideology of de-ideologization and shows that this fig leaf is vulnerable to the storm that will uncover the flaccid, sorry organs that cannot engender well-being and hope in the future.

He shows us that imperialism, the bourgeoisie and such are more than worn-out phrases, that they still exist, whether or not we are aware of them. And, even if you play sleight of hand with those concepts, they're still there to screw up anybody who's in the way when time runs out.

T. B.

Tomás Borge: After a period in which, some say, people didn't pay enough attention to Che's thinking, it now has a central position in Cuba. To what do you attribute this return?

Fidel Castro: Look, Tomás, we've always paid a lot of attention to Che's thinking. I myself have kept his thinking increasingly in mind, ever since we began our process of rectification, long before all those problems arose in the socialist camp and perestroika appeared on the horizon. I remember that we were observing an anniversary of Che's death — I think it was the 20th anniversary — and I spoke at length about Che and all these matters.

My admiration and fellow feeling for Che have grown as I have seen what has happened in the socialist camp, because he was categorically opposed to the use of capitalist methods for the construction of socialism. One of our comrades, an economist, gathered together all of the ideas Che set forth in this regard in his writings and speeches, and he compiled and arranged them. They are of enormous value and should be studied, because I think that the use of those capitalist methods and categories had an alienating influence in the socialist countries.

You were asking about what caused the failure of socialism in those countries.

I think that Che had a prophetic vision when, as early as the first few years of the 1960s, he foresaw all of the drawbacks and consequences of the method that was being used to construct socialism in Eastern Europe.

He said there was no need to resort to those methods and to that capitalist philosophy. At one time, we began to use economic planning and management methods that were copied from the European socialist experience. When those concepts began to prevail in Cuba because of the enormous prestige of the Soviet Union and the other socialist countries and because of the idealistic mistakes we made in the first few years of the Revolution, it created a culture favorable to the appearance and application in Cuba of the methods for the construction of socialism that were being applied in the Soviet Union and other socialist countries. I've always made a distinction between the Soviet Union and the other countries, because socialism wasn't built exclusively with those methods in the Soviet Union. I'm referring mainly to the smaller countries in the socialist camp, because the development programs in the Soviet Union were very powerful, and the main decisions that made the Soviet Union's great economic growth possible weren't associated with income-yield capacity in the capitalist sense or any other such categories. That philosophy was applied in our country. After 10 or 11 years, while we were waiting to see its results, so many deformations and deviations occurred that I had to stop and think and constantly remember Che and his premonition, his rejection of those methods of socialist construction. I think that what has happened in the socialist camp makes Che's economic thinking on the construction of socialism more timely than ever.

When the process of rectification was begun, I encouraged the printing of those books on Che and spread Che's economic thinking — but not for use as a manual, as something infallible, because you shouldn't take any school of political thought or the thinking of any theoretician or politician as something inflexible, as something dogmatic. All my life, I've been the enemy of dogma. We should keep the thinking of the most illustrious politicians and of the most outstanding revolutionaries from becoming dogma, for all thinking corresponds to a given moment, circumstances, amount of information or experience. Thus, things that Lenin may have viewed at one time as correct formulas for dealing with a given circumstance may not be applicable in other, different circumstances or in different times.

The ideas of Marx, Engels, Lenin and Che aren't dogmas — they are brilliant samples of talent and of political, social and revolutionary vision created at a certain time. They are always applicable as long as you don't consider them immutable dogma; to do so would be to take them out of the scientific, political, revolutionary context and make them a matter of religion.

I tried to spread Che's ideas widely when we saw that the Soviet Union and the rest of the socialist camp were taking a different path, that led them farther and farther away from Che's thinking, when they were heading toward ever greater use of the categories and mechanisms of capitalism. In their efforts to improve socialism, they were using larger and larger amounts of the poison that was killing socialism. That's one of the causes of what happened in the socialist camp.

Those were mistakes that we didn't make in our process of rectification. Moreover, we've been very careful about how we carried it out. Naturally, conditions have changed. Right now, we can't do some of the things we had been doing, but we're working methodically and patiently, doing the things we had programmed. It takes more than one, two or three years to rectify mistakes and negative trends that have been in effect for many years. We said that old and new mistakes and negative trends had to be rectified; some were as old as capitalism, and some were new, having arisen within the Revolution or in the era of the revolutionary process. We have rectified many things.

We were talking about rectification in Cuba long before anybody spoke of changes in the Soviet Union — several months before the word "perestroika" came up. Perestroika appeared to be an attempt at rectification, a positive attempt at rectification. That's how we viewed it, though we were aware of many of the mistakes they were making.

When they began talking about putting an end to income that didn't come from work, which was one of the first things that was mentioned when the word "perestroika" appeared, we thought that was marvelous, because we are resolutely opposed to all income that doesn't come from work — the income of speculators, thieves and other corrupt individuals. We even considered that moralizing campaign against alcoholism — realistic or not — to be a splendid thing. When they talked about the accelerated development of the economy with the intensive application of science and technology, it seemed magnificent to us; when they spoke of economic growth on the basis of using intensive rather than extensive methods, many of the things they said seemed excellent. But I want to remind you that the word "rectification" was used in Cuba long before people began talking about perestroika in the Soviet Union, which was after the congress of the Communist Party.

It seemed to me that there was an atmosphere of rectification in the Soviet Union when they first used that word accompanied by a series of ideas and concepts. They didn't talk about wiping out the Party, the Soviet state or socialism. Who would have thought of any such thing? Nobody proclaimed the demise of socialism; rather, they talked about an improved socialism.

In our process of rectification, Tomás, we've been very aware that it was a mistake at certain times to apply the experience of other socialist countries here in the construction of socialism and in economic planning and management. I've already explained the causes for this and the circumstances that favored it.

Tomás Borge: "De-ideologization" is one of the terms used most frequently nowadays. What reflections does that word evoke?
Fidel Castro: The world is more ideologized than ever, now, because they're trying to impose the ideology of capitalism, imperialism and neoliberalism and wipe off the political map any ideology that doesn't coincide with it. I'm convinced that it's all a great farce, an enormous lie.

For example, the principle of peaceful coexistence was always a norm for the relations between states, no matter what their economic, political and social systems. That's dozens of years old. If, by "de-ideologization," you mean the development of relations between countries and the search for peace and cooperation in spite of ideological differences, the revolutionary movement has been pushing for that for a long time — nothing about it is new. I don't know what people mean by that term, unless it's to try to eliminate everything that contradicts or diverges in any way from the ideology of imperialism and capitalism.

Tomás Borge: Do you believe that neoliberalism is simply an economic doctrine, or is it a political project that seeks to perpetuate the present economic order?

Fidel Castro: It seeks not only to perpetuate it but to make it even more cruel and unfair and to so order the world that it serves the interests of the United States and the other developed capitalist countries.

Neoliberalism is the ideology of imperialism in its phase of world hegemony — it seeks to impose its ideas on other countries. Nevertheless, the United States itself doesn't apply those ideas: it tells the Latin American and other Third World countries that they shouldn't have budgetary deficits, yet its own budgetary deficit amounts to $400 billion, which makes it a machine sucking in hard currency from all over the world. It says there shouldn't be any trade deficits, yet it has the largest trade deficit in the world. It says protectionist policies should be eliminated, yet it has more than anybody else. It says there shouldn't be any subsidies for industry or agriculture, yet it is the first country to subsidize its industry and agriculture. And it says there shouldn't be any restrictions on free trade, yet it uses free trade conditions to serve its own ends.

What do these policies of the United States and the International Monetary Fund amount to? It's as if they held a soccer game — to speak of a well-known sport — between the Olympic champions and a kindergarten team, with the same rules applying to both. They tell the kindergarten team that, to score, they have to get the ball to the other goal, 50 meters down the field from the center line — I think it's 50 meters from the center line to the goal. And they tell the Olympic champions the same thing: to score, they have to get the ball to the other goal, 50 meters down the field from the center line. It would be fairer to say that, if the kindergarten team got the ball 20 centimeters down the field, that would be equivalent to a goal, while the Olympic champions would have to get it 50 meters down the field to score — that is, it would be fairer if they played with different rules. In this case, they're organizing things with exactly the same rules applying to everybody: free trade and no protection for national industry.

That is, the United States says, "Apply all of the economic measures that not even we apply consistently; clear away all of the obstacles and limitations so you can become developed and receive capital." It then plunders those countries with high interest rates and the profits it makes on investments; with the flight of capital; with unequal terms of trade, buying their raw materials cheap and selling them its products at high prices; and through competition in which it has all the advantages through imposing its technology. The forms of plunder are multiplied to the extent to which it imposes these formulas and the Latin American governments accept them.

The negotiating conditions are unequal, too. A mighty power, the United States, has the powerful international economic institutions at its service discussing matters with countries plagued with problems and difficulties, countries that have already been undermined and weakened. Those are the absolute worst conditions for negotiating; the negotiating isn't done in conditions of equality.

That is the policy that the United States is imposing on Latin America. What kind of a future will those peoples have? It will be unbearable. Time will show that it's unbearable and will destroy the current prestige of those capitalist and neoliberal ideas; countries that have more than 400 million inhabitants now and will have 800 million within 25 or 30 years cannot resign themselves to that fate.

The lives and fate of 800 million human beings cannot be sacrificed, ignored or exploited in that way. I see this whenever I talk with other Latin Americans. It really breaks your heart to hear what they say about what's going on in the slums; what's happening to the children, the women and the unemployed; what's happening with education; the growing number of Latin American children who are homeless and have to try to survive in the streets; and what's happening with the health situation in all of those countries, that now have AIDS and other diseases from the developed countries, in addition to diseases such as cholera, that the developed countries don't have but which has scourged Latin America in recent years.

Faced with that situation, Latin Americans are becoming truly desperate. I'm talking not about political leaders but about professionals, intellectuals, writers, scientists, doctors, teachers and engineers. I've attended many meetings in which those people have spoken — meetings of doctors, teachers, mothers and women in general — and the situation they describe now, Tomás, is much more terrible, more desperate and hopeless, than the one they described at the beginning of our Revolution, over 30 years ago. I can see this. It's only a matter of time, because this policy is creating an enormous time bomb in Latin America. Are we going to wait for it to explode before we start thinking about these problems? There is no future for us, and I think the politicians and all progressives and democrats in Latin America have a basic duty to pay it all the attention it requires, or we will all become slaves. The history of the discovery and conquest will be repeated. Perhaps 500 years from now, people will be recalling the moment when that neoliberal policy was imposed.

I don't think that will happen. Within 30 years, there will be more than 800 million of us, and you can't exterminate 800 million people like flies — 800 million people can't be killed or annihilated. The history of the discovery and conquest won't be repeated, with the hundreds of millions of us who are the new "Indians" being "discovered," conquered, taught and educated.

CHAPTER 5

The 500th anniversary

Celebrated and discussed until we're sick of it, the 500th anniversary of the colonization of the Americas has entered our daily lives with scandalous, sensational advertising as just another product of consumer society.

But, in spite of all the stratagems that have been designed to limit our ability to think for ourselves, the black legend remains, a part of our memories of extermination and plunder.

To begin with, we Latin Americans have nothing to do with all that bell ringing in European cathedrals, nor should we sit down on sidewalks or paths to moan, evoking our sorrows.

It is true that the Europeans humiliated us, imposed their languages on us — including beautiful Castilian and sweet-sounding Portuguese — and made us believe in a single God. But we can say that, in one sense, they didn't conquer us. We are still Indians, blacks and mestizos. We aren't like them, but are different — neither better nor worse, but different. We are the survivors of a shipwreck that took place centuries ago and are determined to build our own caravels.

Our struggle is a very serious one which most Europeans don't take seriously. Latin America is preparing for battles that aren't at all like that children's game or that eyesore that was the Berlin Wall.

The repercussions of what happened in the Soviet Union will be judged small when compared with the racket that will be made when the wall that separates North and South comes down: the wall between cholesterol and anemia. In our countries, we tend to use and abuse metaphors and bloodbaths.

The recent histories of Nicaragua and El Salvador, to cite examples from the Central American arena, contain so much of this that, in the end, reason seems to have triumphed, with the creation of the theoretical bases for peace and stability.

The violence in Colombia is a rehash of other battles, which the European mass media attribute to the unrestrainable imagination of our writers. And I don't want to even think about what will happen in Peru, to mention just one of our volcanoes that's about to erupt.

Recent events in Venezuela show, for the nth time, that democracy without social justice is worth no more than our devalued currencies. Political democracy is an empty formality if not accompanied by economic democracy.

For centuries, nurtured by the colonies, the Europeans dedicated themselves to creating a luxurious solitude. They erected monuments of iron and words, mastered continents and symphonies and invented machinery and philosophical systems.

The citizens of Europe took great pains to build an enormous stage upon which the actors could be seen from far away; they have everything they need and more, but most of them don't have a chance of knowing themselves and of communicating among themselves.

However, I have known Europeans — many of them, luckily — who are sensitive to our peoples and feel genuine affection for us. They make us very grateful, and, someday, they will be in the majority in the Old Continent.

The curtain should come down so that this play that we call history may be seen by the actors in it; so the dialogue and foreseeable conclusion may be changed; and, above all, so that new actors from other parts of the world may have speaking parts.

Here in Latin America, we are trying to create new human beings — rescuing them from disdain and torment, giving them a crown of laurel leaves and making them a god — while over there, in Europe, they praise postmodernism.

In the Old Continent, little is said about the New World, these lands that Martí called "Our America" and the homeland of "natural man." And, when people do speak of it, it is with pity and remorse, or with solidarity laced with charity — though sometimes with true solidarity.

In many cases, especially at the institutional level, self-centered solidarity prevails: concern with these distant, God-forsaken worlds in order to feel virtuous, just like giving charity to the poor at the doors of churches.

Europe is growing more unrecognizable, even for those who live there. Therefore, I suspect that we Latin Americans will someday "discover" Europe, though not for colonial purposes.

We will "discover" it without the sword or the cross, without seeking gold or a fountain of eternal youth, but simply with the desire to incorporate its children in the socialization of freedom.

The most valuable of the initiatives of the 500th anniversary, because of its prospective harvest, has been the Ibero-American Summit Conference, which was held in Guadalajara in July 1991 and continued in Madrid in July 1992.

With its determination to tackle specific global and sectoral tasks, the forum of heads of state or government of our community may be a good remedy for the premature old age of our part of the world. "The immense contribution that the indigenous peoples have made to the development and plurality of our societies" was recognized there, and the "pledge to support their socioeconomic well-being and the obligation to respect their rights and cultural identity" was reiterated.

They even proposed that a fund be created to promote the development of our Indians, "to make it possible to solve the native peoples' pressing problems, away from the principle of reservations or paternalistic compensation."

This was similar to the autonomy process that the Sandinista Revolution promoted along Nicaragua's Caribbean coast. And, if our hopes bear fruit, Spain, Portugal and the rest of developed Europe will contribute to this.

Generally speaking, however, our relations with the former colonizers are still distant, formal and filled with rhetoric. For the Europeans, the 500th anniversary celebrations don't constitute an act of repentance and aren't even aimed at making amends.

Hundreds of millions of dollars are being spent to observe the anniversary, while our people are starving to death. Our lands, the victims of ethnocide, are receiving no solidarity or compensation. The happiest — and the saddest — thing is that the Europeans are celebrating what they consider their great achievements: the strengthening of European unity, the victory over Communism, the resurgence of a new Germany and verbal paternalism with Latin America.

We, however, are going to take this opportunity, 500 years after

Columbus reached these coasts, to once again promote reflection on the national liberation of our peoples, chained by backwardness and balkanization.

I haven't sought to be cruel. At worst, I'm only giving vent to a 500-year-old resentment and inviting the Europeans to join us Latin Americans in seeking mutual understanding.

We'll be waiting for them here — not only in October 1992 but every October until the end of time — among birds and tigers, for them to discover that this is not a zoo but the promised land.

With equanimity and respect for the anniversary, with justice and objectivity, Fidel Castro makes some unexpected observations about this happy yet sad anniversary, that has resurrected caravels and calvaries before people's eyes.

T. B.

Tomás Borge: Fidel, what are your views on the 500th anniversary of what some call the discovery of the Americas, others call the meeting of two cultures and still others call who knows what, to whose observance we are summoned this year?

Fidel Castro: Look, Tomás, I'm not against the observance of the 500th anniversary of Christopher Columbus's arrival in the Americas, and much less am I against acknowledging the great historic importance of that event. What I have stated, simply, is that this commemoration shouldn't become a mere whitewash job for the so-called discovery and its consequences — rather, it should be a critical commemoration of that event.

You can't deny Columbus's tremendous merit, from both a scientific and human point of view. Columbus carried out a veritable feat, demonstrating not only his personal courage but also his intuition and skill in making excellent use of what little experience had been amassed in terms of sea navigation. Moreover, we shouldn't judge the men of that time by today's ideas, and Columbus was a man of his time. He arrived in the Americas with the cross and the sword to take possession of all he found; he took slaves, but, even so, we shouldn't judge him by the ethical precepts of our time. I admit that I admire Columbus as a scientist and as a very daring man.

The incontrovertible historical facts show, however, that the "discovery" accompanied phenomena that were quite terrible for the American peoples — such as the conquest, eviction from their land, the destruction of their civilizations and the extermination of the indigenous peoples. How can we close our eyes to the fact that wars, indiscriminate slaughter, brutal exploitation and even diseases imported from Europe wiped out tens of millions of human beings in one of the bloodiest and most tragic processes recorded in the history of humanity?

The "discovery" was also associated with modern slavery, the loathsome traffic in human beings by virtue of which, for more than 300 years, countless millions of Africans were forcibly torn from their homelands and subjected to a regimen of brutal labor on the plantations and in the mines of the Americas.

I am amazed that so many people in the world, and especially in our countries, keep on using the term "discovery" to refer to the historic event of October 12, 1492. From our American point of view, we can never allow people to talk with implied scorn of the "discovery" of cultures that, in many cases, had already achieved brilliant development. Such people forget, for example, that Tenochtitlán may well have been the most populous city of its time anywhere in the world, including Europe, and that the Incan Empire was one of the most elaborate state organizations of its time. But, even conceding that, with his voyages, Columbus changed the thinking of his world. If it's a matter of "discovery," you must say that Americans and Europeans discovered each other. Above all, the violence and cruelty of the European Conquistadores were "discovered."

Some people get out of this bind by referring piously to the "meeting of two cultures," but that term doesn't seem appropriate to me, either, because it was really the imposition of one culture over another, the crushing of some peoples by others who possessed more advanced military techniques; it was Europe's violent intrusion in the Americas. Perhaps you could call it the 500th anniversary of a tremendous collision of two cultures.

It is true that, in addition to diseases and social ills, the

Americans received some good things from Europe. We Spanish-Americans, for example, received a common language from the Spaniards, thanks to which we communicate easily with one another. The Spaniards also brought certain norms of social organization and juridical principles; and a culture that, though it prevailed, blended both with the one that already existed here and with the one that the Africans brought later on, creating our rich Spanish-American culture. It would be hard to recognize ourselves as the citizens of Our America that we are today and to have common bases for building our peoples' absolutely necessary integration if it hadn't been for the Spanish colonial foundry.

I should also say, to the Spaniards' credit, that, unlike the Anglo-Saxons who colonized the northern part of this hemisphere, they mixed with the Indians and Africans. Even though that mixture was often stained with violence against indigenous women, the fact is that it occurred and was of key importance in creating the composition of many of our present nations.

I have maintained that, in this commemoration, we shouldn't ignore the extremely critical viewpoint of the representatives of the indigenous American communities; we should pay attention to their demands. Only thus would the commemoration be balanced and fair — by affirming the positive aspects and acknowledging the negative ones.

These are historical events, and, as such, they can be analyzed with historical objectivity. It is hardly necessary to tell you that none of this is inspired by any feelings of hatred toward any country in particular — much less, Spain — as some enemies of Cuba once tried to make people think, for their own purposes. We may well be more closely linked to Spain by ties of blood and history than any other Spanish-American country. Rather, this critical approach is inspired by the defense of certain key values in the Spanish spirit that are undeniable.

Frankly, as a Cuban, I'm glad that Cuba was colonized by Spaniards rather than by racist Europeans, because our people's marvelous mixture came from that kind of colonization. Cubans unquestionably inherited many of the Spaniards' national characteristics, including their rebelliousness and fighting spirit.

That spirit is what led us to wage a long war — first against colonialism and then against neocolonialism, underdevelopment and all the other manifestations of the plunder and exploitation to which the peoples of what has been called the Third World were subjected. We Cubans have had to fight hard for nearly a century, not only in terms of theory and ideas but also in practice against the United States' plans to rule our country. Therefore, our concepts of nationalism and patriotism and our opposition to colonialism and hegemony are very strong.

There is a fact that we cannot ignore: in the northern part of our hemisphere, there is a powerful empire that, historically, has conducted its relations with the countries of Our America on the basis of aggression, intervention, interference in all spheres, domination, the exploitation of our resources, arrogance and the promotion of division among us. Therefore, we look positively on everything that helps to strengthen our countries' sense of unity, everything that serves to counter the divisions fomented by our arrogant northern neighbor.

Therefore, I reiterate that the observance of the 500th anniversary may prove useful, to the extent that it serves to bring out the cultural, historical and ethnic values that all Latin American countries have in common, together with our shared traditions and customs. Everything that helps to enhance those shared values forms a shield that protects us against those who threaten us. To the extent that we can reaffirm our awareness of our identity and increase our peoples' spirit of unity, we will be defending our right to have a place in the world of the 21st century.

Five hundred years ago, a culture was imposed; now, they want to impose a certain way of life on us and control our thinking. In a world that is being pushed toward uniformity and in which the end of history is even being announced as a means of depriving the peoples of their historic awareness, we Latin Americans must have a clear sense of our identity and diversity; proclaim the beginning of a new history of integration; include in it the enormous, silent masses of Indians, blacks, poor people and all who have been pushed aside in our sorrowful republics of which José Martí spoke; and once again make them protagonists in history — which is far from having ended and in which they are still being exploited.

Therefore, we must see to it that the observance of the 500th anniversary doesn't simply become a whitewash. If that were to happen, we would be condoning the conquest, colonization, slavery and the dissolution of the awareness of our identity and history. Now, when some people once again want to "discover" and conquer us, we must have ideological weapons with which to defend ourselves against those real dangers.

All of the solemnity and enthusiasm that we may contribute to this commemoration shouldn't lead us to ignore the negative historical processes that were associated with the "discovery" and haven't entirely disappeared as yet. We cannot forget that we are being subjected to forms of neocolonialism that are sometimes worse than the old colonial methods, that unequal terms of trade, the foreign debt, the destruction of our environment and the plunder of our resources by the developed world still continue.

Now, there are more of us "Indians" — 400 million of us — and we are more productive than in the past. All of the gold and silver that Spain extracted from the Americas in three centuries of colonial exploitation is worth less than the wealth that leaves our countries now every year.

For us Latin Americans, the best commemoration would unquestionably be a 500th anniversary in which there isn't any foreign debt, unequal terms of trade have been eliminated and our peoples have the possibility for development and hope. Only thus would this commemoration have a truly revolutionary dimension and positive value for our peoples and for the entire world.

That, Tomás, is what I can tell you in general terms in response to your question. We could go on talking about this for a long time, but what I've said sums up my basic thinking on this subject — which, I repeat, is based on the need for the observance of this anniversary to be a critical one rather than simply a whitewash.

CHAPTER 6

Democracy

The word "democracy," of Greek origin, means power or strength of the people. Rather than being horrified by it, bankers and generals have taken it over with extraordinary brazenness and admirable persuasion.

Democracy is based on the principle of the subordination of the minority to the majority and on the recognition of freedom and equality in terms of civil rights. We are accustomed to see it only in its formal terms, divorced from social reality. It is said that, when you get right down to it, democracy is determined by the owners of the wealth, who also control the mass media and distribute the resources, and that it is subject to historical events. This is what Fidel Castro thinks.

When they feel safe and it's in their interests, capitalists are proud of democracy and use it as a surgical tool or as acupuncture needles for exercising political control. Then come the constitutionalist euphorias, the rhetoric defending representative institutions, and praise of elections and formal political freedoms.

Generally speaking, all possibility of using these mechanisms is energetically and subtly denied to the dispossessed. The promises of rebuilding democracy cannot hide the crumbs and torn and dirty clothing of that society.

The democratic apparatus of our republics is structured to inhibit political activity by the masses and to limit the workers' participation in decision making. Cuba has a democracy of another kind, that doesn't please the big monopolies.

Latin America has many ragged, lawless children, but this is not the case in Cuba, nor, to some extent, was it so in Nicaragua for a short time.

It didn't surprise me that Fidel began his remarks on this subject *with a quote from Lincoln. Using it as a starting point, he set forth his view of democracy and the nature of democratic life in Cuba. He also suggested the possibility of political changes in harmony with the essence, the raison d'etre, of the socialist revolution.*

T. B.

Tomás Borge: What does democracy mean to you, Fidel?

Fidel Castro: Very briefly, as Lincoln once defined it, democracy is government of the people, by the people and for the people.

For me, democracy means that governments are closely linked to the people, arise from the people, have the support of the people and devote themselves entirely to working and struggling for the people and the people's interests. Democracy implies the defense of all the rights of citizens, including the right to independence, freedom, national dignity and honor. For me, democracy means fraternity and true equality among men and women and equal opportunities for all men and women, for every human being who is born.

Capitalist bourgeois democracy doesn't contain any of those elements. How can they can talk of democracy in a country where a minority has immense fortunes and others have nothing? What kind of equality or fraternity can exist between a beggar and a millionaire? What rights do the poor, the dispossessed and the exploited have? In capitalism, it's an old trick, an old tale, an old story. What they have done is establish a system of domination with all the resources of wealth, publicity and everything else in the hands of a class that maintains discrimination and excludes the rest of society from any real participation and from any real possibility of exercising their rights.

People used to cite Greek democracy as an example, democracy from the classical age of Greece. Athens, which was the prototype of democracy, had 40,000 citizens — men, women and children — and 90,000 slaves. Around 35,000 of the slaves worked in workshops and in agriculture, 20,000 were women who were house slaves, 10,000 were children who provided various services and 25,000 worked in mining. For every free man, woman and child in Athens, there were more than two slaves. Even the great historians and philosophers had slaves — I'm not criticizing them, because they were products of their society. A slave wasn't anything; they were human beings who could be bought and sold, or even killed.

I wonder, really, what great difference there was between that society and this society that imperialism and its supporters are trying to exalt. For example, I think of Martí — Martí never conceived of that form of democracy. I think of Bolívar — Bolívar never conceived of that form of democracy for the Latin American countries. To the contrary, he criticized attempts to imitate the forms of political organization of France or the United States.

Those great thinkers of Our America never identified themselves with the kind of democracy that the imperialists wanted to impose or had imposed or are trying to impose on us — and with which they have weakened our societies, breaking them up into a thousand pieces, so they can't solve problems. There is no real participation by the people in that kind of democracy, because opinions are manipulated to a great extent by the mass media. People's criteria and decisions are almost completely influenced by advertising, propaganda and what are called "scientific" methods for influencing how people think.

Many of those so-called democratic forms are a quite disgusting show. You can see that money is a decisive factor in the kind of electoral propaganda in which they engage. In the United States, those who don't have resources can't set themselves any political goals, because they're excluded and eliminated. Over $100 million, $200 million and $300 million have been spent on advertising in some electoral campaigns in Latin America. What kind of democracy is that, in which they use the same methods in seeking votes as in trying to get consumers to drink Coca-Cola, to smoke a certain brand of cigarettes, to use a certain kind of perfume or to use any other product? That's how those campaigns are run.

I don't believe it's really necessary to have more than one party, either. For our countries, and especially for a country such as Cuba, one of the most important things is unity — of our forces and of our country — which has made it possible for us to stand firm against all of the United States' threats and acts of aggression. How could our country have stood firm if it had been split up in 10 pieces?

What is usually called democracy is a mechanism that serves as a tool; it's a system that includes not only the political but also the economic and social ideas of imperialism. For me, democracy is something else.

I think that our system is incomparably more democratic than any other, incomparably more democratic than the system in the United States.

You can't say that democracy arose in Athens. People have spoken of Athens, but it had a class society. I think that the exploitation of one human by another must disappear before you can have real democracy. I'm absolutely convinced of that. As long as there is enormous inequality among human beings, there isn't — there can't be — any democracy.

Tomás Borge: What about subordination to another country? Must that disappear, too, before democracy can exist? How can a country that is dependent be democratic?

Fidel Castro: It can't be democratic, nor can a country be democratic that has social differences, inequality and social injustice or one where millions of people are unemployed, lack medical attention or have no schools. How can you talk of democracy when the vast majority of the people haven't even finished the sixth grade — I'm talking about the Third World countries, now — and people don't have access to wealth, well-being or anything else? In those conditions, there can't be any kind of democracy, because there isn't any participation by the people or any cooperation among them. What those countries have, really, is permanent civil war — their societies are divided into countless parts, so the nations can't tackle basic problems, and the whole system becomes a tool of imperialism for maintaining its domination.

Tomás Borge: It is said that a diversity of political parties is an artifice aimed at dividing the peoples...

Fidel Castro: I think that that is true in the conditions of our country, and I'd go farther and say that the last 200 years of Latin American history have demonstrated the utter failure of all those concepts. I also think that the present circumstances in Latin America, which are so terrible in all spheres, also demonstrate the failure of such concepts. The form of political organization should promote unity, if possible.

Tomás Borge: Can the Latin American peoples attain the forms of democracy that exist in Europe?

Fidel Castro: The situations of the European and Third World countries aren't comparable. The European countries are rich and developed; they have established certain political forms and achieved certain standards of living by exploiting and plundering the rest of the world. They amassed enormous wealth that they took from the Third World, from the colonies and neocolonized countries, and they have achieved a passable standard of living. They invented procedures for maintaining a sort of social peace based on redistributing some of the wealth to alleviate the worst consequences of class society and the system of capitalist exploitation, and to calm the masses of the poorest and dispossessed. They have managed to establish a system — I'm not going to call it a single-party system — of single-class government. They've established a ruling class that, using different methods (which include some differences of opinion within the capitalist system), has created a political situation in which nothing threatens its system. Its members are rich and live in peace; nobody threatens or attacks them. They live in conditions that are completely different from those in Third World countries — and especially those in a country such as Cuba, which is subjected to a blockade, threats of aggression and imperialism's ongoing hostility, which forces us to make a truly incredible effort to survive. These conditions aren't at all similar to those in Europe.

Moreover, frequently, citizens of the European countries don't even engage in the hardest work. Who does that work in Europe? Africans — Algerians and people from black Africa — Turks and Asians, people from all over. They're the ones who do the construction work and all the hardest jobs on the land, raising olives, tomatoes and other crops. Immigrants usually do that work. It's a new form of slavery — more benign than the slavery of the poor and disinherited in the age of Greece, but still a form of exploitation and slavery.

There may be a difference of opinion, but it's a difference of opinion within the system, whose continued existence is ensured by the monopoly on all means of communication, all money, all wealth and all the power of the state. This is the only way a system of that kind can continue to exist.

Now there is a system of exploitation at both the national and international levels. Look how the United Nations reflects Western concepts. What democracy is there in the United Nations? Nearly 180 independent countries are members of the United Nations — since the Soviet Union disintegrated, that number has increased, I don't know to how many — but only five countries have the right of veto. If all the members except one of those that have the right of veto agree on something in the United Nations, that single country in the Security Council can veto what all the rest want. And they call that democracy! What democracy is there at the world level? Can that be defended?

Some of those countries, with 50 million inhabitants, have the right to veto what the rest of the world wants, yet other countries, such as India, with 800 million inhabitants, don't have the right of veto. Analyze this from the standpoint of population: Brazil, with 150 million inhabitants, doesn't have the right of veto, nor does Nigeria, with more than 100 million inhabitants. Several countries have over 100 million inhabitants: Indonesia is one, but it doesn't have the right of veto and isn't a permanent member of the Security Council.

Look at it from the economic point of view: some countries with tremendous economic weight, such as Japan, aren't permanent members of the Security Council and don't have the right of veto. Germany also has a large population and particularly enormous economic clout, but it doesn't have the right of veto. That is, some anachronistic, truly prehistoric privileges are maintained within the United Nations. This is why I often say that, if you want to talk about democracy, you should begin by democratizing the United Nations.

There isn't any democracy at the national or international levels. Changes should be made in the structures of the United Nations, seeking more democratic formulas for representing the peoples, but all it takes is a vote against by even one of those countries that have the eternal right of veto, and you can put paid to the introduction of reforms there. The United States is gradually gaining control of the United Nations, turning the mechanisms of the United Nations and the Security Council into tools for its domination — which is a far cry from democratizing it. This situation is really cause for concern.

Tomás Borge: You say that Cuba's system is more democratic than any other. Why?

Fidel Castro: True democracy cannot exist in the midst of social inequality, in the midst of social injustice, in societies divided between rich and poor. Democracy can exist only in socialism. The highest form of democracy will be communism, but we haven't reached that yet.

I admit that these so-called democratic forms are more humane than the forms of domination the exploiting classes imposed in other eras; they are more advanced than absolute monarchies and feudalism and are even more advanced than they were to some extent in the last century; I don't deny that. There's a little more distribution of wealth and there are policies for alleviating the most critical situations of the poor and exploited, with unemployment compensation that protects part of the population and some welfare. But all that is a consequence of fear of social revolution and much of that is a consequence of the rise of socialism.

Since the rise of socialism, the bourgeois societies have been very concerned about trying to hold back the revolutionary movement and social change; they've been trying to limit excessive poverty, and, since they have enormous resources, they can redistribute some of them. France, England, Spain, the United States and Germany can afford to give some unemployment compensation and offer some welfare projects; they have the resources with which to improve the situation of the neediest classes. But what resources do the Third World countries have? What resources do the Latin American countries have for providing unemployment compensation, improving living conditions, improving health, improving education and easing the life of the poor?

Just look at Latin America: the more they talk about democracy, the more slums there are, and tens of millions of people are illiterate, tens of millions of people are unemployed and tens of millions of people have no medical care. And the International Monetary Fund's measures and those of other, similar institutions make this situation worse, not better. In some countries in Latin America, 10 percent of the population receives over 50 percent of the income. How can you talk about democracy in such conditions?

Moreover, imperialism and the other highly developed capitalist countries have established a world system of exploitation and domination. They support one another financially when any of them has a crisis: the yen, the deutsche mark and the pound sterling come to the rescue of the dollar if the dollar has problems, and the pound sterling and the franc come to the rescue of the lira. The system has been set up to provide mutual support, but who helps out the Third World? When the Argentine austral, the Bolivian peso, the Mexican peso, the Venezuelan bolívar or the currency of any other Third World country has problems, who comes to its aid? Who comes to the rescue? Who supports it?

So, there isn't any worldwide political or economic democracy; there's no true national democracy — no political or economic democracy and no equality.

All of those bourgeois capitalist societies were established following the ideology of the French Revolution — that, as Marxists and Marx himself always maintained, was a great step forward compared to the feudal regime. That Revolution proclaimed the basic principles of liberty, equality and fraternity. What real liberty can exist in those class societies? What liberty do the poor and dispossessed have? What equality and fraternity can exist in a class society?

Capitalist society cannot be democratic, because it is the

supreme expression of the savage struggle, lack of equality and fraternity among people. Therefore, I can't conceive of democracy within the capitalist system. I can conceive of democracy only within the socialist system, in which it may take one form or another, to suit the conditions of a given country. In a world in which peace truly reigns, democracy can take more forms of expression in a fair society. In a world in which the world hegemony of the mightiest imperialist power reigns and the peoples' sovereignty, territorial integrity and independence are threatened, democracy won't have many different forms of expression.

We have found our form of expression of democracy, and we believe that it suits our conditions ideally. Its effectiveness has been shown for more than 30 years, and I think that no country could have stood firm against the blockade, the threats, the acts of aggression and the terrible blows of the toppling of the socialist camp and the disappearance of the Soviet Union if its people weren't politically aware and united — not split into a thousand parts. Therefore, unity is the main thing for us.

This is also in line with Martí's principles, because Martí created a party for carrying out the revolution. We, too, have a party to defend the Revolution.

In general terms, this is what I can tell you. I can sum it up as follows: True democracy cannot exist within capitalism; democracy can exist only within socialism.

Tomás Borge: Is that why the Eastern European countries collapsed — because there wasn't any democracy?
Fidel Castro: The Eastern European countries were basically an artificial creation; they weren't the product of revolutionary changes.

I think, however, that several rights were guaranteed in the European socialist countries that aren't guaranteed in the Western capitalist countries. I think that, in spite of all their deficiencies, the European socialist countries had a thousand aspects that were much more humane than what we see in other parts of the world.

The main cause for the collapse of the European socialist countries was the absence of a true revolution. In addition, as I see it, there were countless mistakes in leadership and an enormous gap between the leaders and the masses, between the leaders and the people — either because the political leaders never managed to achieve identification with the people or because they lost the identification that existed at one time.

Those processes were also victims of ideological weaknesses and negligence, victims of the use of capitalist mechanisms in promoting development. This would take a long time to explain. Che went into it in the first few years of the Revolution and was resolutely opposed to the application of those mechanisms. The fact that consumer societies were being idealized and consumption became almost the main goal had a lot to do with it; they drew away from their revolutionary, political standards and principles and practically made consumption the main aim of society.

Tomás, you know very well that, when the Sandinista government was having a hard time, subjected to U.S. aggression and the blockade, many of those countries didn't express even the least international solidarity or willingness to make sacrifices for Nicaragua. That is, their internationalist awareness and spirit had disappeared. Solidarity with other peoples, which is one of the most inspiring elements of Marxist-Leninist thinking and of revolutionary thinking as a whole, had disappeared.

Great social inequality also appeared and grew. The ideological influence of the West, through its consumer societies and advertising, grew ever greater. That combination of factors was weakening and undermining those societies and creating the conditions for imperialism to achieve its goal of boring from within, which was its avowed strategy. Note that it put forward a differentiated policy toward the socialist countries, helping those that accepted these things and that had certain characteristics. That weakening facilitated the conspiracy of the United States and the rest of the West to destroy the socialist camp.

What wrecked the European socialist countries wasn't lack of democracy but lack of revolutionary awareness, revolutionary principles and truly revolutionary methods. That's what I think.

If lack of democracy in the world were the preamble to social change, capitalism would have disappeared already, because capitalism was developed on the basis of force and repression. It still uses them: when students take to the streets in protest demonstrations, special police forces repress them with tear gas and riot shields; when workers go on strike and hold demonstrations, the police repress them; and, when slum dwellers declare a strike, as they did recently in England, the police repress them, too. I'm not talking about Third World countries, but European countries. Reports keep coming in of police repression of students, workers and other citizens.

A capitalist regime is maintained on the basis of force — a highly sophisticated, well-organized force. It employs force not only to prevent social change but also to put down people's protests.

In the more than 30 years since the triumph of the Revolution, we've never had any episodes of this kind, with the army and police repressing students, workers or others. That has never happened in Cuba since the Revolution, because, in our country, we have achieved unity, a sense of identity, and very close ties between the government and the people.

Why is this possible here but not in the much-touted European democracies? Why is it that, in those countries, mounted police, fire hoses, tear gas and dogs are used against the people constantly — there's a report of this nearly every day — yet such things haven't happened in our country even once since the Revolution? In which of the two systems is there more fraternity, unity and solidarity? In which of the two systems is there more violence used to keep the system functioning?

When you analyze this problem from all angles, you see that you can't call what they have democracy. As I have said, if lack of democracy were to cause governments to collapse, the capitalist system would have collapsed a long time ago.

Tomás Borge: There is talk in the various media — even by leaders of progressive parties — of the need to broaden democracy in Cuba. As I understand it, they're referring mainly to the possibility of letting those whose opinions differ from the government organize and have their own means of expression.

Fidel Castro: Look, Tomás, nobody can deny that, because of the political-ideological blow that resulted from the disaster of the socialist countries, there is a lot of confusion in the international progressive movement. There is also quite a lot of opportunism in the progressive movement, with people trying to backpedal like mad for having once sympathized with Marxist-Leninist ideas, leftist ideas or what have you. All this is going on right now. Imperialist propaganda as well as recent setbacks in the revolutionary movement have created a lot of confusion.

Moreover, many people don't really know how democracy functions in our country, how our government functions, what principles are embodied in the Constitution, how elections work in our country and how candidates are elected — that is, how people are nominated, who nominates them and who elects our country's representatives. There is considerable ignorance about our country's democracy and its democratic institutions.

I'm not going to say that our democracy is perfect. I couldn't claim that. Nor can we afford to make idealistic mistakes in the present situation, which contains bigger threats, greater risks and worse difficulties than ever. We aren't going to play around with our country's independence and security or with the Revolution, pretending that circumstances are ideal and dreaming up idealized forms of leadership and political organization that can't be applied in the present circumstances. However, we are making a great effort to improve our political system and democracy.

We aren't against people having opinions that differ from ours. In Cuba, the main thing is the battle between the nation — the Cuban people — and imperialism. There aren't any third positions here — you are either with the Revolution or against it, nobody's neutral. We won't help reactionary, counter-revolutionary, imperialist views to spread among our people, because we aren't going to help imperialism or create conditions that are propitious for imperialism's acts of aggression.

Let the economic blockade against our country, the United States' threats and attacks, the campaigns against Cuba and the war against Cuba end, and then, in those different conditions, we might even seek different political formulas for our country. But we can't do this in the midst of a decisive battle, a battle of life or death, in which we are confronting the ideas of our nation's and people's enemies — the enemies of the Revolution and of our country's independence. Not only the existence of the Revolution but also that of the Cuban nation has been at stake. We aren't going to be so stupid as to give means of expression to those who want to destroy the Revolution and our country. That's how we see it. Here, there won't be any mass media for the counter-revolutionaries, because the mass media in our country belong to the people and are at the service of the people; they will never be at the service of the counterrevolution and imperialism.

If the blockade and all the rest of it ends, then we will be able to consider another form of political leadership for our country, both in theory and in practice. But it won't have anything to do with bourgeois democracy, because true democracy is government of the people, by the people and for the people — a government in which all the people participate.

In no country are the people and the government more closely identified than in Cuba. Our people can say, "I am the state," because our people have the power — the people have the weapons to defend their interests. Our people are armed. We exist because we have defended ourselves.

Everywhere, throughout history, the government has been the embodiment of strength. Now, the Cuban government is the embodiment of the people's strength, and the people are indeed strong. What would become of the Cuban government without that strength? What would become of the Cuban government if the people weren't armed? It couldn't exist.

Since we're talking about democracy, we issue a challenge. In our country, the people not only have the right to vote but also have the right to bear arms: farmers, workers and students, all the people, have the right to bear arms. What would happen in Europe if the workers, students and all the other sectors that are constantly repressed whenever they demand something or mobilize for something were armed? What would happen in any of those societies of exploiters and exploited if the people were armed? This is why I say that nowhere else in the world are the people and government so closely identified as in our country. I think this is eloquent proof of the essence of democracy and of the fact that democracy can exist only in a fair social system, a socialist system.

Tomás Borge: People talk about the contradiction between renewal and defense...
Fidel Castro: What contradiction, Tomás?

Tomás Borge: How far can the changes, the renovations, go without endangering your country's defense? You were talking about some changes, weren't you?
Fidel Castro: Yes, we are improving People's Power.

Tomás Borge: What efforts are you making in that direction?
Fidel Castro: Some of the things we have created are very advanced, and we aren't going to touch them. We're improving People's Power: for example, we've created 93 People's Councils in Havana.

Havana has 15 municipalities; it's a city with a population of 2.1 million. We've created People's Councils at a level closer to the base than the municipalities and they are composed of delegates from each electoral district. Those People's Councils have immense power. Their members are the delegates nominated and directly elected by the people, and the mass organizations and main production centers and service entities participate in them. The head of each People's Council represents the people, the municipal government, the province and the central government. The Councils have very great powers and are closely linked to the industrial and commercial districts of the city and other areas where services are provided. It's a new institution that we have created in the process of improving our system.

The main step we're taking is that of instituting the direct election of deputies to the National Assembly, the most important body of governmental power.

It isn't that the method used up until now wasn't democratic, but it was an indirect election, with citizens electing the delegates from each electoral district to the Municipal Assemblies of People's Power who then elected the members of the Provincial Assemblies of People's Power, who in turn elected the members of the National Assembly of People's Power. That has been changed now, with the people directly electing the members of the Provincial Assemblies and deputies to the National Assembly. That improves our system of People's Power.

Tomás Borge: Can people who aren't members of the Communist Party be candidates?

Fidel Castro: Yes, of course. Many of the delegates aren't Party members. Not many people outside Cuba are familiar with our nominating system. Who does the nominating? Not the Party.

This is a much more democratic method than the multi-party system, because it's the people living in a given area, all the citizens in an electoral district, who nominate the candidates — from two to eight candidates, one of whom is elected.

The people living in each electoral district hold an assembly and say, "We think that, because of such-and-such qualities or such-and-so characteristics, Joe Blow should be the representative of this electoral district, be elected delegate of this electoral district," and they nominate him.

Nobody asks anybody if they are a Party member or not; the Party can't interfere in that process. The Party can't launch a political campaign for any of the people who have been nominated as the electoral district's delegate. The Party doesn't participate in choosing who will be nominated; it's the citizens, not the Party, who make the nominations, and the delegate from the electoral district is the candidate who receives more than 50 percent of the votes. If there are several candidates and none of them gets more than 50 percent of the votes, the two who received the most votes have a run-off election; that's how our delegates from the electoral districts are elected.

This is extremely democratic — more democratic than the multi-party system, because, under that system, it's the parties, not the people, that nominate the candidates, and the ones they put at the top of the list are the ones who are sure to be elected. So it's the party, not the people, who elect the deputy or whatever, because the party nominates the candidates and makes up the list of candidates, so you can know almost mathematically who the representatives in the legislative branch will be.

In our case, it's the people, not the Party or parties, who

nominate the candidates and elect the winners. What other country has a system like this or a more democratic system?

Another thing: with the reform of the Constitution we're planning to make, those delegates from the electoral districts, who are nominated and elected by the people, will nominate but not elect the candidates running for deputy to the National Assembly. Thus, the Party won't nominate the candidates running for Deputy to the National Assembly, either; the delegates from the electoral districts, who are nominated and elected by the people, will do so. The Party neither nominates the delegates from the electoral districts nor will nominate the deputies to the National Assembly. Is there a more democratic procedure anywhere?

The people are free to nominate anybody they want as delegates from the electoral districts, and those delegates are free to nominate anybody they want, too. This is what I'm proposing, and the rest of the Party leaders support it. We hope this is the way it will be. Several commissions are studying all these things, but, I repeat, this is what I'm proposing in this process of improving People's Power and our democracy.

We give the people, not parties, the power to nominate and elect candidates. There can't be any procedure in practice that's more democratic. We'll keep on improving our government, and we'll have the most democratic procedure in the world.

Naturally, this assumes that we have the support of the majority. The people in each electoral district have been nominating and electing their delegates ever since we drew up the Constitution. If the majority were against the Revolution, the Revolution would lose power with this procedure. This is the form we've drawn up for elections in our one-party system.

It's logical that, when the people nominate or select candidates, they try to choose the best ones, and many (though not all) of the best people are in the Party. Many good people, with great merits, aren't in the Party. For some of them, Party membership would be one more drain on their energy, a great sacrifice. Being a Party member means being committed to greater effort, to much more sacrifice.

CHAPTER 7

Cuba and the United States

When the Cuban people took power, revolutionaries all over the world sensed the magnitude of the change, the burial of geographical determinism and the appearance of the most charismatic, eloquent leader of modern times.

Cuba threw itself into impassioned solidarity with causes that were or seemed good. It helped so many countries and so many human beings this way that countless numbers of them are — or should be — grateful and ready to express that gratitude in Cuba's present circumstances.

Cuba donated oil and guitar strings. It gave blood for those injured in earthquakes and for those wounded on the field of battle in Latin America and Africa.

Cuba sang lullabies, boleros, love songs and songs of battle to the listening peoples. It provided metaphors and medicines, meeting every need unhesitatingly. Fidel Castro created that style.

If the Cuban Revolution were to disappear, it would be a devastating blow to our peoples' hopes. It would also be disastrous for the other governments in this hemisphere, for they would see their independence and sovereignty curtailed by the United States. This would also increase the danger of a return by reactionary military figures — though many in the Americas aren't reactionary — now lying in wait for more propitious times.

Cuba is life insurance for the growing independence of the Latin American countries as a whole. In that context, it wasn't by chance that, contrary to all forecasts, the Ibero-American presidents who met in

Guadalajara in July 1991 — without Washington's presence in the wings — were respectful to Cuba and the right of our countries to self-determination.

I have talked about this with several leaders from the region, many of them members of the Permanent Conference of Latin American and Caribbean Political Parties (COPPPAL), and most of them agree with this point of view.

The most beautiful, admirable aspect of Cuba has been its generosity.

We should repay at least a tenth of what it has done for us, and do so immediately. I think that we can be useful in denouncing the inhuman U.S. blockade. We must convince international public opinion and especially public opinion in the United States to get the government of that country to change the archaic, irrational and cruel policy it is applying against Cuba. That's the only decent thing to do.

The time will arrive in the not too distant future when the United States will come to its senses and become respectful, when its terrible pretentiousness will end, when it will stop acting like an evil stepmother and become a sister.

When this happens, it will become a country worthy of the large numbers of its citizens who enroll in the most noble causes and will also be worthy of the respect and affection of other peoples.

Will the United States acknowledge the injustice of the war against Nicaragua, which cost all Nicaraguans rivers of blood? Will the United States, someday, engage in self-criticism for its attempts to assassinate Fidel Castro? Will it repent for having bombed Qaddafi's home? Will it reveal who was responsible for Kennedy's assassination?

Those questions will be answered only when imperialism has disappeared.

T. B.

Tomás Borge: From this perspective, I ask: Will Bush manage to be reelected President of the United States? Do you foresee any substantial changes in U.S. political life in the immediate future?
Fidel Castro: I think it's very probable that Bush will be reelected,

in spite of the economic recession in the United States, because he has all the resources of power and maneuverability and doesn't have any strong opposition. Right now, I can't see any leaders in the Democratic Party who could defeat Bush in an election. I don't think the Democratic political leaders are clear enough on the main world problems and those of the United States. Any opposition that can win the election in the United States and make changes in the country's present trends would have to have very clear views on the main world problems and convey an attractive message to the people of the United States about their own interests.

You know how those things work in that country: it has a single party composed of two sections with very similar concepts, political ideas, goals and purposes but different names. In the United States, there are two capitalist parties that squabble over power, two parties that have been tools of imperialism throughout this century and that continue to be so.

Naturally, this doesn't deny that there are very intelligent and very capable people. It doesn't deny the possibility that, at times, individuals may have tremendous influence on the course of the United States and even save it from collapse — there's the case of Franklin Delano Roosevelt. I believe Roosevelt was a truly talented man who saved U.S. capitalism from one of its worst crises and who can be considered a great statesman because of what he did on the domestic scene, pulling the country out of economic crisis. It was the same in the international arena, in the struggle against fascism, the struggle against Hitler's Germany: the struggle against another imperialism that was more warlike and more aggressive (though never as warlike and aggressive as U.S. imperialism itself is now).

Tomás Borge: Can Kennedy be included among those great statesmen?

Fidel Castro: Kennedy can be included among the great figures, but not among the great statesmen. He was a very intelligent man, an outstanding personality, but he didn't have the opportunity to express himself as a great statesman. He died very young, during his first term.

I think that Kennedy had outstanding personal qualities, but he was still very inexperienced when he took office. He still let himself be swayed by what others thought and sometimes by emotion. He made mistakes, such as launching the Bay of Pigs invasion. He had a good idea, an idea with positive aspects, in the Alliance for Progress, which was an intelligent attempt to suppress the factors that could become a culture fomenting revolution in Latin America. It offered economic and social reforms to alleviate the needs of the poorest — the typical response of capitalism — out of fear that the Cuban Revolution would be copied. The Alliance for Progress was inspired by fear of the Cuban Revolution and the desire to keep Cuba's experience from being repeated in other countries. The Alliance for Progress was developed after the Bay of Pigs invasion was defeated.

Kennedy had a constructive position and was intelligent. He was courageous when he didn't go along with the idea of the United States intervening directly in Cuba — a thing that would have taken a terrible toll, both for them and for us. He was courageous when he acknowledged his responsibility for the Bay of Pigs invasion, even though Eisenhower and Nixon had organized the invasion before Kennedy won the election and took office.

He continued an aggressive policy against Cuba that led to our taking defensive measures. This caused the October Missile Crisis. He was responsible for that, but it should also be said that he recognized some facts about the Soviet Union, the reality of the Soviet Union and the destruction the Soviet Union had suffered. He made a speech in favor of peace, in which he perhaps began to develop as a statesman.

Kennedy died at the height of his prestige and authority after the October Missile Crisis, when his influence inside the United States had grown and he could have done something constructive in terms of international policy.

I didn't mention another of Kennedy's mistakes. He was very eager to test the effectiveness of the Green Berets, the elite troops he organized and sent to Vietnam. So, the other mistake that Kennedy made was to get into the war in Vietnam, and he didn't have time to rectify that, to express his ability as an intelligent man, as a statesman. That's the most objective analysis I can make of Kennedy.

Tomás Borge: Following the making of the film "JFK", there has been a lot of talk all over the world concerning his assassination and even suggestions about reopening the investigation. What do you think about Kennedy's assassination, and who do you think his assassins probably were?

Fidel Castro: The day the report came in that there had been an assassination attempt against Kennedy in Dallas, I was meeting with Jean Daniel, a French journalist, who had just spent several hours with Kennedy in Washington. Kennedy had spoken very frankly with him about the tragic situation caused by the October Missile Crisis and had asked him to come and see me, to talk with me to find out what I thought, and then go back and see him in Washington. Unquestionably, Kennedy was thinking something over. That gesture and that visit interested us.

Daniel came, and I told him, "Let's get out of the city so we won't be bothered and can talk in peace," and I took him to Varadero. We were there, talking — it was around noon — when the report came in, so he didn't have a chance to go back and talk with Kennedy again. We were very upset by his death. Kennedy was our adversary, and we were adversaries of Kennedy. If you're any kind of a gentleman, you're sorry if your adversary has been assassinated and you've lost him — you miss him. The way they killed him hurt, and it hurt that his death occurred at a time when he had just made a speech in favor of peace and seemed to be attaining international stature, a few months after the October Missile Crisis, and when he had even sent a kind of emissary or scout — we could call him that — to our country after the talk he had with that journalist.

Kennedy was our adversary, but we had to acknowledge that he was an intelligent man, with good qualities. The news of Kennedy's death made me bitter — not at all pleased, even though he had taken harsh measures against Cuba, had wronged us and had attacked us. That was my own reaction, as I've always said.

Now, you're also adding what my initial reaction was when

the first reports came in.

Tomás Borge: No; what do you think now?

Fidel Castro: All right, but first I'm going to talk about my initial reaction. It seemed to me that a lot of things were strange. The shots with a rifle with a telescopic sight were the most surprising. How could an individual have hit a moving target with the precision and speed with which Kennedy was shot, at that distance from the place where Oswald was said to have been?

I have a lot of experience using telescopic sights, because I trained those who came on board the *Granma* [in 1956]. We trained in shooting and became quite skilled and precise. During our voyage, I adjusted nearly all of those rifles so they would shoot at targets 600 meters away. We had more than 50 of them with us on the *Granma*. On land or at sea, I adjusted all of the telescopic sight rifles, and I shot them tens of thousands of times, against all kinds of targets, in that period.

We practised against stationary and moving targets, both from a prone position and standing, with the rifles at our shoulders. In 1963, those memories were very recent, and it seemed extremely difficult — almost impossible — for anyone to fire so many shots against a moving target in such a short time — and do so with such precision that Kennedy was seriously injured three times. It seemed to me it would have been much easier to do that with a normal sight, a Lyman, which has a dot inside a circle — the system used in the U.S.-made Garand rifles and also the U.S.-made M-1 carbines and the Belgian FAL rifles.

It would have been much easier to carry out an action of that kind with an automatic rifle without a telescopic sight. When you use a telescopic sight, you have to bring the next bullet up into the breach of the rifle again and get your target back in your sights after you've fired off your first shot. It isn't easy, and it takes time. To prove this, you would have to do some tests and place some good marksmen with telescopic sights at that distance and angle and get them to try to reconstruct the action in the same time as the shots were fired. They could have made that kind of experiment, to see if the thesis that a single individual had fired those shots against Kennedy in that time and with that precision held water. That was the first thing that caught my attention: telescopic sights have a specific use in certain circumstances, mainly against a stationary target, not a moving one. Therefore, I was surprised.

It was even more amazing that the individual arrested and charged with having killed Kennedy was assassinated inside a police station — that was very suspicious. Oswald's background was also strange. He had been in the Soviet Union, had married a Soviet woman and had gone back to the United States. It wasn't clear whether he was an agent or a double agent. That, too, seemed very strange to us.

After all those things happened and his name was released, we checked some files and discovered that an individual of that name who answered to his description had presented himself at our embassy in Mexico and asked for a visa to come to Cuba — I think it was a temporary visa, en route to the Soviet Union. Our personnel turned down his application. Whenever a U.S. citizen spoke of coming here, they were suspicious of his reasons, and they turned him down. I wonder why Oswald wanted to come to Cuba? What interest could there have been for that individual come to Cuba? What would have happened if he had come to Cuba, gone on to the Soviet Union, returned to the United States and killed Kennedy? There were many strange, inexplicable things surrounding that situation. That was my impression.

What did I do? I waited to see what investigations they would make, and they came up with the famous Warren investigation. Then there were books and statements by Kennedy's relatives. None of Kennedy's relatives and none of the intellectuals, writers and journalists close to Kennedy challenged the Warren report. They accepted it, more or less tacitly.

My attitude, then, was that if the people closest to him, the ones who could have challenged the report and those who may have had more information didn't do anything, the investigation may have been carried out well. It was still odd that all of those people close to Kennedy accepted the report practically without protest. That added a lot of confusion to the various theories about Kennedy's death.

Moreover, I don't like to get carried away. I don't like to

make statements that can't be proved. I haven't seen the movie you mentioned. I've heard a lot about it and I would like to see it, but I can't give you an opinion of a movie I've only heard about.

It wouldn't surprise me in the least if it makes some new discoveries about how or why Kennedy was assassinated, because it seemed very odd and abnormal at the time. It wouldn't be correct for me to come up with a theory on that or to begin blaming somebody and make a study of that old problem.

We should also keep in mind that there's a lot of secret information. What is that secret information that the U.S. government decided shouldn't be released until 100 years after Kennedy's death? What could that information be, that has to be kept secret for 100 years? I think that the U.S. government has a responsibility to clear this up.

Tomás Borge: Like the secrets of Our Lady of Fátima.
Fidel Castro: What are the secrets of Our Lady of Fátima?

Tomás Borge: What Our Lady of Fátima told the three little shepherds to whom she appeared, which couldn't be published for 100 years. They say now that she predicted the fall of socialism, that it was one of the secrets kept in a chamber to which the Pope doesn't have access. And now the U.S. government's secrets have to wait 100 years, too.
Fidel Castro: It would be a matter of witchcraft, not religion, to be predicting such things.

Tomás, the U.S. government must have some very important information. Therefore, I think that, in one way, it's a good thing that these matters are being discussed again, because it was never cleared up — yet the Warren Commission report said it was settled. Now that you brought this up, I think I should see the movie, because there's a lot of talk about it and it has unquestionably made an impact on public opinion. But I can't comment on it yet.

Tomás Borge: Cuba's policy in this current situation is to stand firm. It seems that defense spending and activities continue as usual on the island, which indicates foresight in case of possible

U.S. military intervention. Do you think that a dialogue or negotiation may take place between Cuba and the United States within a reasonable period of time? And, if such negotiation is feasible, what would you propose for an agenda?

Fidel Castro: It is true that our military spending hasn't decreased. We have no alternative. It would be absurd, crazy — suicidal — at a moment such as this, when we are standing alone against the empire, without any force or resources other than our own, if we were to make the mistake of failing to look to our defenses. Therefore, the strengthening of our defenses is one of the programs with top priority in the special period and one of the sacrifices that we simply must make. We mustn't commit irresponsible acts that the present and future generations would hold against us.

There is a real danger — a greater one than ever before — because the United States feels that it owns the world and is filled with triumphant crowing and a blind, mystical, fanatical faith in its strength, its might, its sophisticated weapons and its ability to impose its will on any nation.

It is unlikely that the United States will resign itself to and forgive us for the role the Cuban Revolution has played and continues to play. It must be very irritating to it that this tiny country is demonstrating its courage to struggle and ability to stand firm. Thus, before negotiation can become possible, changes must first take place in the thinking of the U.S. leaders, and I'm not at all sure that this will happen in the near future.

The United States thinks that we've had a very hard time since the disappearance of the Soviet Union and the collapse of the socialist camp, because we're waging this battle alone. It thinks that this creates favorable conditions for imposing its policy on us, one way or another.

By saying this, I don't mean that we're fatalists or that we think war with the United States is inevitable. Many U.S. citizens are beginning to question the reasons for the United States' policy of hostility toward Cuba, the economic blockade and the tightening of that blockade — what reason there is for the cruel policy of trying to strangle the economy and starve a small nation such as Cuba into surrender, of trying to increase the people's suffering and force us to our knees. They wonder what the reason for that is, now that there isn't any threat to U.S. security, when the other superpower has disappeared and the "communist threat" has ceased to exist. What possible justification can there be for that policy of hostility against our country, of trying to force us to our knees, of trying to impose its will on us? Many U.S. citizens are beginning to ask these questions, because there is no reason other than an arrogant, insane obsession. Many people are beginning to think this way in the United States, though this doesn't mean that they have any great power or decisive influence.

This is an absurd, inglorious policy for the United States. As it is implemented, it will reflect well on Cuba and Cuba's prestige, because, as hostility increases, growing numbers of people in the world will denounce that policy, and the other Latin American and Third World peoples and others all over the world will express more and more solidarity with Cuba.

U.S. policy-makers should come to the conclusion that this is an inglorious struggle that offers them nothing. What do they want to do with Cuba? Create utter chaos and a war that will last dozens of years? Where does the United States' policy lead? Cuban revolutionaries are never going to surrender but will keep on fighting. No true revolutionaries — and there are hundreds of thousands, millions of us — are going to give up what we have, and you can't crush the determination of millions of people who are ready to fight in any field, under any circumstances. Therefore, the United States' policy toward Cuba doesn't lead anywhere, and, the more it does to hurt us, the greater the prestige of Cuba and the Cuban Revolution will be.

They should change that policy someday. Naturally, we can't expect them to do this immediately — especially in a country where demagogy, political scheming and electoral ambitions generally determine what the politicians do. We'll have to wait who knows how long for them to change their policy — which, I think, would be the smartest thing they could do.

They aren't going to give up their dreams of wiping out the Revolution in our country, but they have two paths open to them: that of hostility and aggression and that of peace with Cuba, respect for Cuba, trying to use other methods to influence Cuba's political life.

We may even be better prepared for standing firm against a policy of aggression than for standing firm against a policy of peace, because that's what we've had to do for more than 30 years. But we aren't afraid of a policy of peace, either. As a matter of principle, we wouldn't be opposed to a policy of peaceful coexistence with the United States. We wouldn't be afraid, and we wouldn't have the right to reject a peace policy because it might be more effective as a tool for the United States to influence us and try to neutralize the Revolution, trying to weaken it and eradicate the revolutionary ideas in Cuba.

So we wouldn't be opposed to a policy of peace. We aren't begging or even asking for such a policy, but if, someday, they should look at their various options and decide on a policy of respect for Cuba and of peace with Cuba — which would have to be without any strings attached, because we couldn't accept any improvement of relations on the basis of concessions of principle or of having others lay down the law concerning what we should do inside our own country — if, someday, they should choose the path of negotiation, we wouldn't oppose it.

You asked me about an agenda. Well, there are a lot of things. First of all, we won't accept peace in order to make concessions of principle. Cuba and the United States may have many interests of various kinds in common that could be the subject of discussion and negotiation, but the first thing we would state is that we aren't about to make any concessions of principle and that any negotiation or arrangement would have to be carried out with absolute respect for our country's sovereignty and independence. That's the main thing.

In addition to the problem of the economic blockade and such things, the Guantánamo Naval Base — a part of our territory that is occupied by force and should be returned to us — would be another topic for negotiation with the United States. Apart from that, we could discuss anything else that anybody wanted to discuss, as long as it was approached in a spirit of respect for principles and for Cuba's sovereignty and independence.

I don't think we have to rush to draw up an agenda yet,

Tomás, because we don't expect that such an agenda will be needed for some time.

Tomás Borge: Do you think the Cuban community in the United States has developed positively and may have some influence on those negotiations in the future?
Fidel Castro: Thus far, the most anti-Cuban, counterrevolutionary elements, those that hate the Cuban Revolution the most, have prevailed and have imposed their policy. But we know that many people don't agree with them and are against the blockade of Cuba. Many people want normal relations to be established between the United States and Cuba. Many people have relatives here and oppose all those things that may make life more difficult for their relatives.

There are forces that oppose the hegemonistic group in the Cuban community abroad, in which shady characters filled with ambition and base interests have gained power that has gone to their heads. I even have the impression that some people in the United States are beginning to get tired of them, with their arrogant, reactionary policy.

It's impossible to imagine what this country would be like if people like that were to try to rule here someday. The Revolution has taught our people not to allow anybody to rule them, and nobody would be able to rule them for at least 100 years — much less turn Cuba into another Puerto Rico or another Miami, a Mecca of drugs, gambling, prostitution and the other vices of U.S. society.

Some grotesque elements have even been deciding how they're going to divide the country up after the triumph of the counterrevolution, how they're going to divide up the land, the factories and everything — as if they wouldn't have to kill us all first before they could attain that ignoble, dastardly aim.

As time goes by, those people are shown up for what they are and have less and less support, even though they have many resources and use terrorist methods. They impose their will not only with their monetary resources, their influence in the U.S. government, their propaganda, but also through terror. Many people in that community are afraid. We don't consider that the

Fidel Castro and Tomás Borge, Managua 1984

Coast watch in Havana during 1962 Cuban Missile Crisis

Ernesto Che Guevara

"I've always managed to take some time from sleep or from work for reading." Fidel Castro in Sierra Maestra during revolutionary war

Celia Sánchez and visiting Vietnamese delegation

Fidel Castro, 1959

Photo by Osvaldo Salas

Fidel Castro and Raúl Castro

people of Cuban origin who live in the United States are a homogeneous community — we distinguish among them, since not all of them are involved in the policy against Cuba or in the plans to destroy the Revolution.

Tomás Borge: Unquestionably, there are serious internal splits among those people. A movie called "Vidas paralelas" (Parallel Lives) should be completed soon, to be shown in movie theaters all over the world. It reflects that contradiction.
Fidel Castro: Where was the movie made?

Tomás Borge: In Venezuela. It's a Cuban-Venezuelan-Spanish co-production.
Fidel Castro: Didn't you have something to do with that movie?

Tomás Borge: I headed the jury that judged scripts, and I voted for this film, which won the prize in the Havana film festival. I'm sure it will be an exceptional movie.
Fidel Castro: I haven't seen it, Tomás. In the last few months, I've had very little time for seeing movies.

Tomás Borge: It hasn't been shown yet; filming has just ended. It's an interesting film related to this topic.
Now, recent events show that the counterrevolution is trying to create a fifth column. To what extent has it managed to achieve this aim?
Fidel Castro: It's highly unlikely that they've managed to set up a fifth column, because they are isolated elements that don't have any roots among the people. They don't have any influence in society, because the main players, the best of the people, all support the Revolution. You've seen the attitude of the workers, farmers, university students and everybody else. The masses support the Revolution, even though they're critical and complain about problems and other things. But, whenever they have to choose between the Revolution and the counterrevolution, between our homeland and its enemies, they don't hesitate. And that spirit has grown stronger in the special period. It's a curious thing, but, in spite of all the efforts the enemy has been making

— which unquestionably have some effect on certain sectors — that spirit has grown stronger.

Five hundred hours of radio broadcasting are directed against our country every week, trying to create discontent, launch counterrevolutionary slogans and promote sabotage and plots against the Revolution. Never before in the history of the world has such a gigantic battery of mass media been installed against any country. They broadcast open calls to sedition, shameless calls to counterrevolution, violating all legal norms; an unprecedented amount of propaganda has been launched against us. All of the empire's resources are now concentrated against Cuba — resources of all kinds, costing tens of billions of dollars every year and involving its information service, its intelligence service and all the other agencies in the main branches of the U.S. government.

Tomás Borge: Does Cuba broadcast radio programs to the United States?

Fidel Castro: Well, that depends. Only recently, we had to make some radio broadcasts in response to the attempt to interfere with our television signal in the middle of the day. We have mainly used interference, not broadcasts.

They have constantly escalated all this. The first thing was the misnamed Radio Martí, followed by Television Martí, which they wanted to introduce here in violation of all international regulations.

We've produced effective interference to block the Television Martí broadcasts and we have also used interference to block Radio Martí. Naturally, they have increased their broadcasts by other means.

We reserve the right to broadcast to the United States. We have the same right to inform listeners in the United States as they have to broadcast information to Cuba, though this isn't the usual way we've replied to those acts of aggression. But we have the means, the right and the determination to do it, if circumstances make this necessary.

CHAPTER 8

Latin America

In Latin America — and probably in the rest of the world, as well — political parties are in the dock. Large sectors of the population have lost faith in leaders, programs, electoral promises and the honesty of elections.

Most of the voters don't vote, and it isn't by chance that some current presidents have been elected as independents: Fujimori and Violeta Barrios de Chamorro, for example. Aristide was elected on the strength of his support for an ethical project.

The political leaders aren't unaware of this credibility crisis. When they meet, they talk about this topic with great concern and are even perplexed.

For their part, the parties on the left have declined, worn out by splintering and doubt. The Latin American left would do well to reflect on the dangers that frighten them and other essential matters rather than concentrate on obtaining a new image.

Looking in the mirror isn't a vain undertaking for Latin American revolutionaries, because a good look might well help cure their distress. The danger of self-contemplation lies in the fact that it may lead to the pleasure of tears and mutual commiseration.

I would like to remind the chorus of leftist lamentation of one essential thing: it isn't our political body that is being buried in Europe. Experience counsels that we act with great realism — but not pragmatism — in these circumstances so as not to lose our balance or our faith.

If the Latin American left persists in being bewildered and indecisive, the possibility of recovering lost ground and adherents will disappear for a long time.

The worst danger for our revolutionary organizations and parties would be to follow in the footsteps of the European left. It is overwhelmed by the defeat of real socialism, the rebirth of fascism and the celebrations in the well-lit zoo of the right.

Our lands, where capitalism has vented its cruelty without worrying overmuch about cosmetics, contain the weakest links in the chain of oppression. The Latin American left now has the historic possibility of acting on its own, free of all extraregional political influences.

Here, the number of the poor is growing daily in absolute terms. The past decade was described as "the lost decade," and this term has become a part of normal usage. Epidemics that we had thought things of the past have even reappeared.

Far from denying what they are, Latin American revolutionaries should reaffirm principles that some consider outdated but which remain in effect because the causes that gave rise to them haven't disappeared. In particular, I'm referring to anti-imperialism, which some "revolutionaries" with unprecedented naiveté — to be charitable — have denied. Our left shouldn't limit its actions to seeking, if possible, a less cruel, fairer capitalism. Our historic goal should continue to be to put an end to that system, which is inhuman in essence.

We should take our general ideas concerning the creation of a new society from the Marxist classics, but our modus operandi should be based on the specific characteristics of our countries and on delightful Latin American and Caribbean thinking, little of which has been published thus far.

Moreover, the Latin American left should do more than concentrate its struggle in civilian society and limit itself to subjecting "the national government" to scrutiny and democratic debate in parties, the press and parliaments.

Renunciation of solidarity would be a substantial part of the Latin American left's irrational self-denial. Of course, we should renew ourselves, but in a diametrically opposite sense. One of the most important actions of reaffirmation of self that I think the left in Our America should carry out consists of reestablishing its sense of the future, renewing its historic optimism.

In spite of the obscene euphoria of the right, the world isn't going back to a former state in sociopolitical terms. The presumed definitive *closing of social utopias — socialism in particular — and the complete triumph of capitalism over any alternative model of social development is more a matter of propaganda than fact.*

If humans prevail, real capitalism will be totally defeated.

For the Latin American left, the main thing is to stand firm. Cuban revolutionaries are doing so, and this now almost unique fact sets an example for others, or is at least worthy of respect and support.

T. B.

Tomás Borge: On the political plane, Fidel, is Latin America advancing, stagnating or retrogressing? In this framework, how would you describe the panorama of the left in our region?

Fidel Castro: Latin America is retrogressing. A little while ago, we were talking about the Alliance for Progress. If you compare Latin America's situation at the time of the Alliance for Progress with its current situation, you can see that the situation now is much more serious. All of the economic and social parameters are worse.

First of all, the area has more than twice as many people as when the Alliance for Progress was created. There is more than twice as much poverty and twice as many slums as when the Alliance for Progress was launched. The health situation is worse, people's income has dropped and there is more unemployment. Social problems have been aggravated to an incredible extent, and, instead of the Alliance for Progress, which was what they promised us then — a very spectacular promise, offering us $20 billion to promote reforms and alleviate Latin America's needs — what we now have is a debt of around $450 billion.

Now, instead of the Alliance for Progress, we have a $450 billion debt and policies of social confrontation imposed by imperialism and its international finance mechanisms. These make the situation of people in Latin America much harder and more terrible. Those policies of social confrontation are resulting in a crisis for the governments and the democratic opening. I differentiate between these forms of democracy which we have been referring and military governments, such as Pinochet's and those of the military rulers in Argentina, Uruguay and other countries. In other words, I make a distinction between the forms of political organization that have been called "democratic" and the governments of Somoza, Stroessner and some other personages in the history of this region. Inexorably, the process of democratic opening will be led into crisis. Very clear, eloquent signs of crisis already exist, resulting from this situation of retrogression in Latin America.

I would also say that the left is experiencing its worst moment in Latin America, its moment of greatest confusion and disorientation. This is understandable, in view of the enormous confusion created in the world by the events that developed in the Soviet Union and that, in the end, destroyed the Soviet Union and the rest of the socialist camp.

It has been a terrible blow for the progressive forces, for all the leftist forces, not only in the political sphere but also in terms of ideology and morale. I think the left is beginning to recover from that trauma, but it hasn't done so fully as yet — far from it. Even so, I think this will be a temporary period.

Tomás Borge: What do you think of the peace agreements that the Farabundo Martí National Liberation Front and the Salvadoran government signed recently?
Fidel Castro: I think those peace agreements are a positive thing, and we're glad that, with everyone's participation, they have achieved a peaceful solution to the war in El Salvador — a war that had gone on for many years, in which the forces on both sides were exhausted and which could have turned into a chronic, interminable war. I think that, in the circumstances, it was wise of the revolutionaries not to have lost the possibility of using that path, if they think that, with their heroic struggle, they can attain their goals by peaceful means and that the conditions are being created for political struggle for those ideals.

Tomás Borge: What do you think of Mexico's role in those negotiations?
Fidel Castro: Mexico played a very positive role, as it has done in

many matters. Mexico wanted an end to that fighting, which was harming the Central American area.

I admire the role the Salvadoran revolutionaries have played, their ability to negotiate and to reach a satisfactory agreement. The future will show how well those agreements are kept, but I think that all of the parties are very committed and that the Salvadoran government won't be able to weasel out of what it has pledged in those agreements.

Tomás Borge: You haven't made many comments about the situation in Nicaragua following the Sandinista Front's electoral defeat...

Fidel Castro: That's right: I haven't said much and would like not to say anything. I don't like analyzing the domestic situation of a country such as Nicaragua, which we have respected and will always respect. I don't think it would be right for me to make judgments about a situation as complex as the one in Nicaragua. I don't know who could benefit from it if I were to do so. What else do you want to ask?

Tomás Borge: Do you think our revolution has come to an end, or is it still alive?

Fidel Castro: I think that no revolution ever comes to an end and that all revolutionaries have the duty to keep its ideas, principles and goals alive. Even if the Sandinista Front were to try to close off prospects for future progress, it wouldn't be able to do so. Nobody controls the future.

I think that you did some great work in your country, effecting great changes and engaging in important social projects that will last. Nobody can wipe them out or suppress them. Therefore, regarding prospects for the future, I think they exist everywhere in the world, in all countries and all peoples, because humanity has no alternative to meeting the future, has no hope but the changes, advances and improvements that the future may bring.

Above all, there are the Nicaraguan people — patriotic, courageous, revolutionary people who fought hard to throw off Somoza's rule, to begin a revolutionary process, to keep struggling in disadvantageous conditions and to recover from setbacks. Therefore, I think that prospects in the most positive sense of the word still exist.

Tomás Borge: After its unexpected electoral defeat, the Sandinista Front has grown. Tens of thousands of Nicaraguans especially young people — have joined its ranks. Moreover, internal democratization has swept our party like a hurricane.

The confrontation in Nicaragua is an expression of the — class struggle and the participation of ethnic communities and social movements. The heart of the confrontation is our determination to reiterate our national liberation and to demand respect for the people's achievements. All of this is now under attack by stupid people who are bound to fail.

Ever since the beginning of our armed actions in the jungles along the Coco River in September 1963, the FSLN has proclaimed its plans for national liberation. We understood that concept — and our position hasn't changed — to be the attainment of independence and the beginning of thorough, radical social transformations.

Starting in July 1979, we did what we could to build a new Nicaragua, and, even though we didn't get as far as we had hoped, we did lay solid bases. Never again in the history of Nicaragua can the masses be kept from having real political participation. Not only the constitution but the whole system of social organizations guarantees this.

I can assure you that Sandinism will continue to be a decisive force in our country's destiny. Depending to a great extent on its internal unity and on respect for revolutionary principles, it will continue to have a key influence. Moreover, I don't rule out the real possibility — because of the great amount of public opinion it reflects — that it will return to power in Nicaragua.

Fidel Castro: I'm glad you have that appreciation and that view of the future.

Tomás Borge: You've mentioned Latin American integration many times. What do you think of that process and the "Bush Initiative"?

Fidel Castro: Look, the Bush Initiative isn't an attempt to promote Latin American integration or even a factor in it — it's an attempt to make Latin America a part of the U.S. economy. Because of the struggle among the emerging great economic powers, the United States wants more than ever to consider Latin America a private preserve serving its interests.

The United States isn't proposing a free trade agreement with the Latin American countries as a bloc. What it's proposing is a free trade agreement country by country, so the Latin American governments won't have any bargaining power. Clearly, it's doing this in order to impose its interests on each and every one of those countries and keep them divided — split — and trying to bring each of the Latin American and Caribbean countries into the U.S. economy individually.

This doesn't have anything to do with the ideas of economic and political integration and unification of Bolívar, Martí and all the others who dreamed of Latin American integration in the past and all those who seek that integration honestly now. Latin America's integration and unity are conceivable only with independence, within the framework of its own interests. Latin America could also become an important economic community. Latin America has no worthy, honorable, independent alternative to economic integration — if it doesn't achieve this, it will have no place in the world of the future.

Politicians and other leaders should become aware of this and see the problem clearly. Often, the specific conditions of each Latin American country limits its maneuverability, its capacity to struggle and work for true integration and to further Latin America's interests.

The United States wants to keep this region split up in dozens of pieces. The United States wants to draw all of those pieces into its economy. In short, it wants to have the U.S. economy swallow up the Latin American countries and maintain its hegemony and its private preserve of Latin America, which is how it views us.

Tomás Borge: One of the political leaders of this region who has worked the most for integration, power stability and other aspects typical of the Latin American democracies is having special difficulties. I'm referring to [Venezuelan President] Carlos Andrés Pérez... What do you think of this?

Fidel Castro: The events in Venezuela are deplorable, but they show the crisis that will be caused by the policy of social confrontation imposed by the United States and the IMF. They're a very clear example of this.

Venezuela is the richest Latin American country. It isn't dependent on sugar. Venezuela has oil, for which it receives over $12 billion a year. Venezuela is a country with enormous energy resources — hydroelectric power as well as oil. It also has enormous mineral resources: iron and bauxite. Nature has endowed it richly. What explanation can the social upheavals in Venezuela have if they aren't proof of what we have been saying about the consequences that policy will bring to Latin America, with the situation becoming more and more unbearable?

If the richest country in this region, the country with the highest per capita income in hard currency in the region, has problems because of a pitiless economic policy imposed from outside, what hope do the rest of the Latin American countries have? What can we expect to happen in the rest of the countries, that don't have Venezuela's vast energy and other natural resources and its immense income? Moreover, Venezuela has some degree of economic and industrial development; it has important industrial resources in diverse fields and a considerable level of technological development. But, even so, it has problems. What clearer proof could there be of what we were saying about the kind of future Latin America faces?

Just compare Venezuela's per capita foreign currency income with that of Cuba — there is no possible comparison. And, if you analyze the extremely small resources with which we have managed to confront this special period without firing anybody, without closing any schools or hospitals, without shutting down any universities and without leaving any citizens unprotected, you will see that we have created conditions that are much more propitious for coping with difficulties than those in the other Latin American countries. It's all a matter of distributing resources fairly. We have little — very little — but we distribute the little we have fairly. If we didn't, our society would burst into a thousand pieces, and nobody would be able to put it together again.

It is very sad to see a sister nation such as Venezuela experiencing these difficulties, but the explanation is obvious — it's clear what factors have caused the crisis, and, naturally, Venezuela isn't the only country with problems.

Tomás Borge: Would you go into more detail about the solidarity shown by people, those whose representatives were here and whom you greeted last night, and also about the position that some Latin American governments have taken toward Cuba? Do you feel isolated, or supported?

Also, I'd like to ask you about the positions that the Socialist International and the Permanent Conference of Latin American and Caribbean Political Parties have adopted toward the Cuban Revolution.

Fidel Castro: Unquestionably, solidarity is growing, and so is friendship. Let's differentiate between the concept of solidarity and that of friendship. Let's apply the concept of solidarity to the peoples. Solidarity is growing all over. That is evident.

Let's use the concept of friendship for the governments. We've noted an increase — I'm not talking about the last few months but years — in the friendship and respect of governments, especially in Latin America. We see that friendship and respect in many countries, even though it must be expressed with great prudence and caution, since the United States will hold it against them and is ever more stringent in repressing any gesture of friendship or cooperation with Cuba.

There is friendship, cooperation — let's call it that — and respect. This is evident, but I don't think we should place a lot of emphasis on this, because the first thing we have to keep in mind is discretion in our international relations so we don't place any government in a ticklish situation or create any problems.

I would like to praise several Latin American figures I met recently. I don't want to name names, but I had friendly contacts with many of the other Latin American leaders at the [1991] Guadalajara meeting. Generally speaking, they were very friendly and respectful toward Cuba. I met some very interesting, intelligent people. It was a stimulating experience.

As a rule, Latin American political leaders are more educated and more capable than before, as I could see in the speeches that many of them gave at Guadalajara, independent of their political differences. For example, there was a general consensus on neoliberal policy — which I didn't share — a kind of euphoria over the "integrationist" ideas of the United States and announcements of the free trade agreements. That has awakened some expectations — which I don't share, either — but I found them to be a group of intelligent men with whom it was possible to talk, people who could understand a message. In the short time available to me, I briefly set forth Cuba's positions, not only in general, but also on specific topics: science, education, health, scientific research, economic integration and a whole series of important things.

Most people had access only to the inaugural addresses. The specific addresses — that I think should have been published, because they contained many interesting points — were never printed. I noted a quality leap in the political leaders there. This doesn't mean that, simply because there was greater personal quality among the political leaders, you should expect this to be expressed in a more efficient policy on Latin American integration or in a more effective general policy. As I already said, all of the Latin American countries are experiencing enormous difficulties, problems that are often greater than the determination, strength and possibilities those political leaders have for solving them. Sometimes, they find themselves in very complex, difficult situations.

As I already told you, I met some very interesting people, and that was stimulating. I don't want to note differences among them — I don't think it would serve any purpose — but I would like to express my great appreciation to Mexico, whose government decided to invite us to that conference. It upheld that decision at all times with a great sense of national independence, even though this could in no way please the United States, and it gave us the opportunity to be there and participate in the conference.

Tomás Borge: I believe that the Guadalajara Summit marked a substantial change in the relations between Latin America and the United States, because it was the first time the heads of state of our countries had met without the U.S. authorities...

Fidel Castro: Yes, it was the first time representatives of the Latin American governments had met without being convoked by, and without the presence of, the U.S. authorities. I think it had great moral and political value and was symbolic of our times. It was one of the positive things that has happened recently, offsetting the many negative things that have also occurred.

Tomás Borge: I mentioned the Permanent Conference of Latin American and Caribbean Political Parties because it issued a communiqué expressing its solidarity with Cuba's defense and territorial integrity. I should point out that around 40 Latin American and Caribbean political parties belong to that agency, and they were unanimous regarding the communiqué...

Fidel Castro: We have good relations with COPPPAL and are very grateful for that declaration to which you've referred. Meetings of the Latin American Parliament and even one that was held in Cuba recently with a large number of deputies from the most diverse political trends participating also issued declarations of solidarity with and support for Cuba, denouncing the blockade. The number of statements, documents and manifestos issued on the problem of the blockade and support for Cuba is growing. That's why I said that solidarity among the peoples is growing and that there is increasing friendship and cooperation with and respect for Cuba by the authorities, important figures, institutions and governments of other countries.

Tomás Borge: I've spoken with many Latin American and European governmental and other political leaders, and nearly all of them have spoken out for the Cuban Revolution. This may be partly because, even though they have ideological and political differences with you, Cuba's disappearance would mean a qualitative increase in U.S. hegemony.

High-ranking leaders of the Socialist International — an organization that was weakened recently but to which many Latin American parties belong — has also gone on record in this regard. The Workers' Party of Brazil, the Socialist Party of Chile, M-19 of Colombia and the Sandinista Front of Nicaragua want to join the Socialist International as full members. Some think that the Socialist International and its progressive positions will be strengthened if their applications for membership are accepted.

There was a lot of discussion in the Sandinista Front in Nicaragua about whether or not to join that international organization. In the end, most of the members of the Sandinista Assembly, our supreme leadership body, voted to join.

The decisions on those organizations' applications will be made soon, during a meeting of the Socialist International.

CHAPTER 9

Survival and development

Once the Latin American and Caribbean colonies won their political independence from Spain, which should have been completed with the unity proposed by Bolívar, their trade fell into the bottomless pit of balkanization. Their structural weakness, political upheavals, continual interference by the United States and other powers, and the lawless, excessive greed of the oligarchies combined to enslave us in backwardness and extreme poverty.

In the last few decades, attempts were made to create trade blocs in the vague hope of industrialization. A slow start to integrating our economies was made recently, however.

Brazil now exports to 10 other South American countries and has sought a closer relationship with Argentina since 1968; in 1991, Brazil, Mexico, Uruguay and Paraguay united, and the Andean Pact, created in 1969, was strengthened. These were important steps toward breaking balkanization and adopting less rigid structures, perhaps with the idea — insisting on imitation — of following the steps of the European Common Market.

The Central American Common Market — formed when the first steps toward the total pacification of the area had been taken — and the Caribbean Community have confirmed the hopes expressed in various documents that the bases for greater economic communion be laid in the coming years.

In spite of the blockade and the fact that it has a different kind of economy, Cuba is gradually increasing its trade with the rest of Latin

America.

Dozens of Latin American, Canadian and European business people have visited the island recently. It isn't good business to kill the goose that lays the golden eggs of sugar. Moreover, Cuba's scientific development — like its tourist development — is opening wide its doors to world trade.

However, we shouldn't lose sight of the enormous difficulties facing this crocodile-shaped island that seems a garden of earthly delights. The difficulties stem from the U.S. blockade and are accentuated by the situation created following the collapse of misnamed "real socialism."

Those difficulties — which Fidel Castro himself acknowledges with healthy sincerity — have put most of the country's production out of joint, so it is now having to tackle serious problems with supplies of oil, imports and spare parts.

The population's basic consumption has also been adversely affected, reduced to levels close to those registered soon after the United States imposed its total trade embargo against the island in 1960. Goods and shortages are shared in Cuba with near-mathematical equity.

It is miraculous how, in the midst of such difficulties, caused by a deliberately perverse policy from abroad as well as objective factors, Cuba continues making social advances in health, education and welfare. It continues to have promising prospects for sustained development, based on projections of the biotechnological industry and tourism and is continuing to promote its ambitious food program for home consumption. Significantly, it still continues to express solidarity with others.

Cuba is maintaining the solidarity with the other Third World peoples that has distinguished it during the last 30 years. Even in the midst of so much need, the Cuban government still offers a large number of scholarships for students from Asia, Africa and other Latin American countries. Every school year, it offers more than 400 scholarships at the technical and university levels for Nicaraguans alone. No one else in our region or in any other part of the world has done this.

Now, Cuba is struggling to preserve the balance between satisfying its basic economic needs and maintaining its ideological principles.

T. B.

Tomás Borge: Now, let's talk about the essential battle the Cuban Revolution is waging for survival in the economic field. What is the immediate situation and what is your strategy?

Fidel Castro: You've covered a lot of ground in just one question, but I'll try to be brief so this interview won't last forever.

We were implementing a series of programs related to the rectification process. That process began in 1986 and we had begun to make really efficient use of our material and human resources in several important programs aimed at solving social problems and promoting economic development.

We were doing many extremely interesting things, even though our resources had already decreased. For example — I'm talking about the situation in 1986, 1987 and 1988 — our hard currency resources had dropped considerably, but we still had a lot of trade with the Soviet Union and the other socialist countries, bringing us a reasonable income in terms of products and other materials. For example, we decided to give a big boost to solving our housing problems; building more child care centers to help working mothers; building trade schools — we already had some, but they weren't top-quality installations — so those young people who dropped out of the normal school system for one reason or another could be trained; and building special schools to meet all of the needs of children with physical disabilities, motor problems, problems of mental retardation, eye problems, hearing problems, retarded mental development — which isn't the same thing as mental retardation — and behavior problems.

As the material base we made large investments in the building materials industry, with its cement, brick, cinder-block, floor-tile, sand, crushed-rock, steel-bar and other plants.

We also made other investments of an economic nature. The food plan had been drawn up before the special period began. So had the plan for developing tourism, biotechnology, the pharmaceutical industry and the state-of-the-art medical equipment industry. There were other economic programs, too, but these were the most strategic ones.

The years 1987, 1988 and 1989 passed, and the Soviet Union and the other socialist countries began to collapse. In my July 26,

1989, speech in Camagüey, I spoke of our determination to struggle, which made many people wonder. Here's what I said:

> Naturally, imperialism and Bush are building castles in the air, based on the difficulties confronting the Soviet Union, the main bulwark of the socialist community. It is true that the Soviet Union is faced with difficulties; that's no secret. The imperialists are hoping that the Soviet Union will disintegrate.
>
> There are difficulties, and tensions and conflicts among the nationalities in the Soviet Union are growing. Other internal tensions are also evident; thousands of coal miners in Siberia, Donetsk and other places have gone on strike. Those reports filled the imperialists and other reactionaries with joy.
>
> Here, reasoning very calmly, as you have to reason with the people, on an anniversary such as today's and at this point in history, we should think and reason. Are we going to stop advancing, stop making this great effort? No, never! Are we going to shut our eyes to reality? No, never! Are we going to act like ostriches and stick our heads in the sand? No, never!
>
> We must be more realistic than ever. We must speak out and warn imperialism that it shouldn't have so many illusions about our Revolution, thinking that our Revolution won't be able to stand firm if there's a catastrophe in the socialist community. If, tomorrow or any other day, we should wake to news that a huge civil war has broken out in the Soviet Union or even that the Soviet Union has disintegrated — something that we hope will never happen — even in those circumstances, Cuba and the Cuban Revolution would keep on struggling and keep on standing firm.

Note this: I said those things two and a half years before the Soviet Union disintegrated. Naturally, all of the programs that we were developing began to be threatened.

I didn't tell you that the food program, which is very

ambitious, had several stages of the utmost importance. One of them concerned the renewal of our water projects program, which had lapsed in that period I told you about, when the economic planning and management methods that were being applied in the other socialist countries were applied here. The development of water projects through those mechanisms was a flop — they didn't become a reality.

The construction sector also went into a slump: projects went on forever and were never completed and of poor quality. It was incredible: a town would be built without streets or a water system, without a nursery and other schools. Before, we had built things in an integrated way, assigning resources and brigades for building a whole town at a time, including schools, child care centers and shopping centers. With the new system, things weren't done that way. With those mechanisms, the education sector had to build the schools, with a construction enterprise of its own that wanted to build schools. The housing sector contracted an enterprise that wanted to build houses to get that done, and it had to do the same to get the water and sewage systems built. Another sector, with another enterprise, was in charge of building child care centers. It was playing at capitalism, really, believing that those mechanisms would work in socialism.

Tomás Borge: Is that when the rectification process began in the construction sector?

Fidel Castro: I could see the disastrous results that the application of those methods was producing in all areas when we began the rectification process. We began by fixing what was wrong in the construction sector, getting it going again, giving it a new organization, applying a series of principles, concepts, ideas, programs and integrated projects. It began to recover.

How did we organize the workers and raise their morale? We went back to creating specialized construction brigades — contingents, which were a new experience in construction and scored some spectacular results: they doubled, tripled and even quadrupled productivity.

We began completing projects. In the past, they hadn't been finished — among other reasons, because the enterprise earned more when it was moving earth and putting component parts of buildings in place, and less when it was giving buildings the finishing touches, because you use machinery for earth-moving and putting prefab sections in place, but the finishing touches are done by hand, with low productivity, so not as much money is involved.

All of those mechanisms led to disaster, to towns that weren't finished, that lacked things, and to projects that weren't completed. A whole series of programs we had been working on, such as the construction of dams, schools, dairies and roads, had begun to suffer when we had applied those imported procedures.

Tomás Borge: How did you solve those pressing problems, then?

Fidel Castro: We replaced those mechanisms that sought to get things done by serving the interests of the various enterprises, which is what happens in capitalism. It had been an attempt to build socialism that way, when, really, socialism is characterized by programming and by viewing as a whole the things to be done.

We began to rectify mistakes, removing obstacles and throwing out wrong concepts. We established the principle that the interests of the enterprise should never prevail over the interests of the country. Sometimes it was better for an enterprise to pay in dollars than in pesos — that is, to rent ships in dollars rather than pay in pesos for our fleet's ships. It may have served the interests of a single enterprise but not necessarily those of the country. We had to rectify a whole series of things without going so far as to suppress that system completely, because we hadn't created an entirely new one, nor could we do so in a matter of months. We couldn't improvise a system, either, but we are already creating the bases for a different system. What we did was amend and rectify many of the aspects of that system that had been in effect since 1975.

I told you about the problems we had in various sectors, problems all over. We began to improve our work. In two or three years, our water projects program really got off the ground and we were building dams, canals and irrigation systems at an impressive rate. Along with that, we built a factory for making central pivot irrigation equipment; it already has the capacity to produce 1,000 of those units a year. That is, we created a whole series of industries and promoted industrial development, apart from the branches I've mentioned, associated with the water projects program.

We developed an ambitious program of engineering systems for land dedicated to sugarcane, called plot irrigation and drainage. We set up 201 construction brigades specializing in sugarcane plot irrigation and drainage systems. That's impressive, an enormous technological revolution.

We created many brigades for building terraces on land used for rice, which doubles rice productivity, just as the plot irrigation and drainage system doubles the productivity of sugarcane. We've been working on all those programs for several years now, organizing our forces, the brigades and the equipment.

We've considerably developed the production of Cuban-made equipment and we were even manufacturing bulldozers, forklifts and trucks. We were making nearly all of the construction equipment used in our country. The construction programs associated with the food plan were advancing and construction in general was also increasing apace.

We were in the midst of that process, Tomás, when the catastrophe hit.

Tomás Borge: Then what happened?
Fidel Castro: Some of those programs in Havana were completed. We built 110 child care centers in Havana in two years. There was a demand for 19,000 places when the program began and we created 24,000 places in two years.

In two and a half years, we built the 24 special schools that Havana needed so it would have a complete program. We built all of the polyclinics that were needed in Havana so all would be in appropriate installations. And we built thousands of family doctor offices with housing for the doctor included. In that same period, we gave a big boost to the family doctor program.

We had a program for creating better university campuses, because some of those buildings were old and inadequate. We were also working on the trade schools.

Some of those programs were completed in Havana, and the housing construction program was given a big boost. We had already created the material base for building from 20,000 to 25,000 housing units a year in Havana alone, and from 80,000 to 100,000 housing units a year in the rest of the country. We reestablished the system of minibrigades, which had also disappeared in that ignominious period of copying the methods used in other places for the construction of socialism.

We were really getting things going when the socialist camp collapsed, followed by the destruction of the Soviet Union. With enormous grief, we were forced to set priorities and begin the "special period in peacetime." Many years earlier, when Reagan began making threats, we had already drawn up our programs and plans for what to do in a special period in time of war, which was equivalent to a total naval blockade, with nothing coming into the country: what to do and how to survive in those circumstances. After we had drawn up those plans for the special period in time of war, we drew up our plans for a special period in peacetime, in which there wouldn't be a total naval blockade but in which our resources would be extremely limited. Suffice it to say that we are working with less than 50 percent of the fuel we used to receive. This really is a special period, though not the same as the special period in time of war.

What did we propose? That, in the special period, we would not only stand firm but also develop. Production of everything that wasn't essential would be reduced. We would practically have to paralyze our social development programs, our programs for building houses, child care centers, special schools, trade schools and university installations. We are keeping some of them up at a reduced rate, such as the trade schools, but we had to suspend most of those extremely ambitious, inspiring programs of social development.

In any case, we were sure that our education could improve every year with what we had already accumulated, because we had nearly 300,000 teachers. We even had a reserve of teachers who could give classes while thousands of other teachers took upgrading courses. We were sure that our health programs could continue to be improved as our human resources increased, with each new group doing even better work and all that work being based on scientific advances. That is, the fact that we had to halt our social programs didn't mean that we were resigning ourselves to lowering quality in medical services, education, sports, culture and many other spheres.

The housing programs had to go by the board. This doesn't mean that all work on housing stopped — rather, all new housing would have to be built in strategic places, such as agricultural communities, to provide housing for a permanent work force to take over from the people mobilized for two-week periods and from the members of contingents. There are several priority programs for which some housing construction continues, but, in essence, the original program (of building 100,000 housing units) had to be cut back drastically, to less than 20 percent of what we had been doing.

So, just when we were preparing to solve large social problems, that situation arose. We said, "Well, the social programs will have to be sacrificed; our economic programs — many aspects of production — will have to be curtailed, but not the essential ones." We stopped distributing household appliances, because, if we aren't going to have fuel for electricity, what's the point of distributing air conditioners or more TVs or other household appliances?

In 1991, when we still had trade agreements with the Soviet Union, it paid us 500 rubles per ton of sugar and it was going to supply us with 10 million tons of petroleum — though it didn't supply the full amount. In 1991, we had to make some considerable cutbacks and suspend purchases of household appliances. And this may last for years.

We had to make great cutbacks, Tomás, but, at the same time, we maintained our priority programs: the programs related to biotechnology, the pharmaceutical industry and the medical equipment industry, all of which are advancing full speed ahead; the program related to tourism, which is in full development; and the food program, which is the first priority. This emphasis on the food program is in spite of some quite serious limitations in the projects for building dams, canals and irrigation systems and in the projects of engineering systems in sugarcane and rice, which we have had to nearly halt while we get everything reorganized and get some fuel — we know exactly how much — so we can resume those projects that support the food program. Our scientific programs continued to be developed as usual. These programs are the strategic pillars of our development in this phase.

Tomás Borge: When did you give a big boost to participation by foreign capital and technology?

Fidel Castro: We took a number of steps in our desperate search for outside resources. Some of those programs, such as in tourism, had been carried out in part in association with foreign capital. We opened up the possibility of using foreign capital and investments in those areas where we had neither the capital nor the technology nor the markets — not only in tourism but also in other investment areas, in which foreigners contributed technology, capital and markets.

But that wasn't all. Associations would also be formed in areas where the foreign partner contributed the market or the technology or the capital — in certain areas, in order to increase exports or reduce the cost of absolutely necessary investments. We used our own resources whenever we could, but, very practically, we decided to open up possibilities for investments by foreign capital in a series of branches, sectors and factories, with associations of many kinds, from those related to the ownership of the enterprise to trading associations. We paid a lot of attention to this, analyzing what was advisable in each case. In reality, we didn't have enough capital or foreign markets.

Tomás Borge: Petroleum, for example...

Fidel Castro: Yes, petroleum is an example. We didn't have the capital or technologies we needed for offshore oil drilling, so we had to either form associations with foreign firms for the exploration and exploitation of offshore oil deposits or renounce all hope of increasing our national production of fuel. There was no other way of doing it.

In the past, we had done such exploration and exploitation with Soviet cooperation and Soviet technology. Now, we didn't have Soviet cooperation or resources or technology; the only thing we could do was join with foreign capital.

Where similar conditions have existed, we haven't hesitated to establish that kind of association, just as we know very clearly where we don't have to do this. Generally speaking, we don't need a foreign partner to run an agricultural enterprise or to keep a sugar mill going or to do many other things. We try to maintain all of the areas that are essentially for domestic consumption with our own resources and with strictly Cuban enterprises.

Sometimes, associations can be formed in the agricultural sphere with enterprises that have markets, since we don't even have a distribution network. In such cases, we establish a trading association. Foreign firms can participate by supplying us with inputs to be paid for out of profits, out of the income obtained from exports and from the trading asssociation.

We have studied all possibilities, case by case, in detail. We've established rules and are applying them. We don't do everything with such associations. In some areas, we're doing practically everything with our own resources. In tourism, we're doing part of it with our own resources and part with foreign capital. We're developing the biotechnological industry, the pharmaceutical industry and the medical equipment industry exclusively with our own resources. These last three are some of the most strategic. We're carrying on scientific research almost exclusively with our own resources. For us, the essential thing isn't just to survive but also to develop, apart from the privations to which we may be subjected for an undetermined length of time.

Tomás Borge: How have you planned the distribution of resources?

Fidel Castro: As a matter of principle, as I said, resources must be shared among all. No citizen may be left jobless. If raw materials are lacking and there is nowhere for a worker to be placed productively, they won't be cut off. We will guarantee a large part of their wage. Nobody will be left without support. That's the difference between what we're doing and policies of social confrontation. The policies of social confrontation that the United States and the International Monetary Fund recommend — which throw millions of men and women out of work and into poverty and hunger — constitute an extremely brutal violation of human rights. We don't apply policies of social confrontation — what we've done is ration nearly everything. There is a great surplus of money in circulation. The total of wages, pensions and other income is greater than the amount of merchandise and services we offer, but it doesn't adversely affect the people's access to essentials, because those products are guaranteed at a set price and are reserved for them. In the future, as the situation is normalized, we will have to get that excess money out of circulation by producing things that aren't so essential and selling them at high prices. Generally speaking, the markets offering produce off the ration card at higher prices have been closed. We couldn't maintain them in these conditions of the special period, even though some nonessential products may still be sold that way.

This is how we have been holding out and tackling this situation. What our country is doing with the few resources it has is truly miraculous. We have applied more restrictions than any other Latin American country and have been deprived of more resources than any other Latin American country, but we haven't closed any schools, hospitals, polyclinics or medical services at all, and we haven't thrown anybody out of work with no pay.

And that's not all. We provide a job or economic support for every university graduate and the same for every graduate of a technological institute. We are creating a reserve of cadres, scientists, technicians and everything else, ready to be called upon when we need them. See what a difference there is in how we're tackling the economic crisis and problems.

No other country has been forced to make the restrictions we have had to make. How have we managed to do this? With the people's understanding and cooperation. How are we carrying out these programs? With the people's cooperation. You've seen this on the tour we made.

CHAPTER 10

Advances in medicine

Since 1981, the Cuban government has been developing biotechnology as its main scientific and technological activity, beginning its spectacular advances with the production of human leukocytic alpha interferon.

In a short time, the production of that biomolecule was stabilized, and it immediately began to be used in medical practice to control and treat viral diseases, such as type 2 dengue and acute hemorrhagic conjunctivitis.

By January 1982, Cuba had created a Biological Research Center, an institution that undertook larger-scale production of alpha and gamma human interferons, both in the conventional way and by recombinant means.

Between 1982 and 1986, it produced monoclonal antibodies and gene fragments, developed new diagnostic methods and acquired advanced knowledge about genetic engineering, virology, tissue cultures and fermentation.

With the creation of the Center of Genetic Engineering and Biotechnology, Cuba acquired capacities for applying the most advanced techniques of modern biology from the laboratory up to industry.

The center has dozens of buildings surrounded by gardens, and its equipment uses a technology that is used only in a few industrialized countries, apart from here.

Young people in green uniforms who came across me in the hall crowded around smiling to support the statements made by their director, Dr. Manuel Limonta, who seems to be both the younger brother of Albertico Limonta and one of Asimov's characters.

It may be indiscreet of me to say this, but they spoke of the possibility of changing the size of fish and, in the most extraordinary *milking in history, of introducing therapeutic substances in milk.*

Four hundred Cuban scientists are working on how to obtain proteins, hormones, vaccines, diagnostic means, hybrids, model animals, energy, biomass, plants, fertilizers, knowledge about the cell genetics of higher organisms and enzymes of restriction and modification.

Another scientific pole of Cuban biotechnology, the National Scientific Research Center, produces polycosanole, better known as PPG, a product believed to have more than the proverbial seven virtues.

Since this medicine produces magical changes in physical and sexual activity and doesn't have any notable side effects, it is supposed that, within a few years, it will be consumed in quantities similar to aspirin.

Fidel Castro has confidence in biotechnology and the pharmaceutical industry. He believes that this will be the key to his country's development — even more important than sugar, though he didn't say anything about halting sugar production.

In spite of all his office work, planning and discussions, the Cuban leader often visits the laboratories and projects to swap ideas.

He isn't amazed when the scientists, working to protect health, offer theses that seem to be a surrealistic dialogue between science and fiction.

T. B.

Tomás Borge: Which of the products made in the biotechnological laboratories and the pharmaceutical industry are the most important?

Fidel Castro: We have many important things, some of which are new and made only in our country, but I'll mention some of them. One of the most outstanding is the antimeningococic type B vaccine, the only one of its kind in the world, which is impressively efficient.

We've obtained Epidermal Growth Factor, which one or two transnational enterprises also make. We've been developing it for some time now through genetic engineering and it's also very efficient against burns.

Streptokinase, a product that we've obtained through genetic engineering and is much cheaper than the kind obtained through other procedures, is very effective for halting heart attacks and preventing necrosis of the cardiac muscles adversely affected by heart attacks. It is a truly impressive advance.

The vaccine against type B viral hepatitis is of high quality and is very effective. And there are many other lines that aren't as important.

We're working with monoclonal antibodies, developing them quickly; they serve diagnostic or therapeutic purposes. We've developed several kinds of interferon. We've been developing blood derivatives, such as Intacglobin, which is tremendously effective against infection, especially in newborn babies who have low defenses against certain diseases. It is a product that comes from blood and is very effective.

We're producing specific gamma globulins, including one against meningococcic meningitis, which we have made from the serum of people who have been vaccinated. You collect the antibodies a person has, and you can fight the disease by using the specific gamma globulin.

One of the most important products we have developed is for combating cholesterol; it's a natural product that's very effective, and I think it has great possibilities. Its trade name is Ateromixol, but we call it PPG — those were the first initials by which it was known, not its trade name. It's a very effective product, and we're already using it in Cuba. It has many possibilities associated with circulation, cardiac diseases and circulatory diseases and a lot of other qualities I don't want to go into now because we're still in the research phase.

There are many other medicines and we'll keep on creating new ones, working at great speed in the search for new vaccines, new products. Now, we're working intensively on a vaccine against cholera.

Tomás Borge: Some of the people who use it say that PPG increases interest in sex. Is that true?

Fidel Castro: Well, PPG is miraculous in that, too, because of its influence in improving the general tone of the organism. It's really a friend of lovers, but we aren't putting it on the market for that purpose yet; we're working on the corresponding medical records. We've made countless tests and have an enormous amount of information. When you draw up records for a certain purpose, you can see the influence it has on collateral problems. I don't want to talk a lot about this yet, and I don't want to turn this interview into promotion for some of these products.

We know a lot about this product. I've told you a little. I prefer to say little about it — just say that, using it as a starting point, we can create a series of medicines that have magnificent properties. We've finished some records on old people — I'm talking about people whose average age is 80 or over — and its effects are impressive with regard to several parameters.

Tomás Borge: So PPG is also a geriatric product...

Fidel Castro: Yes, it is. We're working very carefully on all these things; we don't want to jump the gun. Right now, we're putting it on the market only as a medicine for combating cholesterol, but our research is very advanced and quite complete concerning the effects it has on another series of diseases associated with circulation. In short, it rejuvenates. That's all I'm going to say; I said this much because you asked, but we don't talk a lot about things that are still being developed.

Tomás Borge: Then let's talk about other products...

Fidel Castro: I was saying that we're working on a vaccine against cholera and I think we'll have results soon. The researchers are very optimistic about the possibility of finding an efficient vaccine against that disease; the one that's used now is less than 50 percent efficient and its protection doesn't last long.

We're working to develop a vaccine against meningoencephalitis caused by type B influenza hemophile; that's another very aggressive bacterium that causes meningitis. Since we've practically eradicated type B meningococcic meningitis, we are now trying to eliminate that other meningitis caused by that hemophile, another bacterium that has a relatively high incidence in our country and which is very aggressive and very lethal.

We're developing that vaccine as quickly as we can for our own use, and we're quite advanced. Soon, before we have the vaccine, we'll have a medicine with which to fight that disease; it will considerably increase the survival rate and also help with therapy against the disease. It's one of the intermediary steps in the production of the vaccine.

Tomás Borge: Have Cuban scientists worked in the search for a vaccine against AIDS?
Fidel Castro: We're working on a vaccine against AIDS, but many other people all over the world are working on it, too. We're also trying to find other kinds of vaccines for combating diverse diseases.

It's an enormous, virgin field, in which more talent is required than economic investments. We already have many talented people, thanks to the educational effort the Revolution made, and that investment in talent is the main element in the intensive, accelerated, successful development of research in this field.

Tomás Borge: People say that the revolution in physics and chemistry was followed by development in some European countries, Japan and the United States. If the syllogism applies, do you also foresee development after a biotechnical revolution?
Fidel Castro: Yes, of course. Biotechnology has become one of the basic elements in development. It's used in so many things, Tomás.

We're using biotechnology to produce new varieties of plants. We're using it, through tissue cultures, to develop plant seeds.

For example, we're developing banana plantations at a tremendous rate; we can do this because we aren't dependent on the natural reproduction of bananas. One banana plant of a given quality can give you four offshoots. Using tissue cultures, that same banana plant can give you 40,000 or 50,000 scions. In laboratories, you can reproduce it as quickly as you want. The same can be said of pineapples and sugarcane, when you're seeking varieties that are resistent to plagues and diseases and varieties with higher sugar yields and other qualities. You can do these things quickly with tissue cultures.

With biotechnology, we're developing biofertilizers, bacteria that fertilize the plants, that take nitrogen from the air and give it to the plants either in association with them or together with the soil or with the organic matter in the soil. We're working hard to develop biopesticides — natural pesticides, not chemical ones — through biotechnological processes.

Tomás Borge: This influences the food program, doesn't it?
Fidel Castro: In our food program, where we lack fertilizers or pesticides, we're making intensive use of biofertilizers or biopesticides, plant stimulants or root multipliers, so they can capture a much higher percentage of the elements in the soil. That is applied biotechnology.

We've already developed some elements of biotechnological origin for multiplying the extraction of oil from our oil wells. We're in the experimental phase in this, but the initial results are very encouraging. We've obtained those products by means of cultures in fermenting machines, not chemical synthesis, thanks to the discovery and selection of certain bacteria that produce that element — that, in this case, is of biological rather than chemical origin by means of synthesis. That is, biotechnology has applications even in industrial processes, in mining and oil, which is a very important resource.

We have great possibilities for using biotechnology in the sugar industry, to use less of certain chemical components and to seek higher sugar yields and greater efficiency in our sugar mills. There's no limit to the fields in which biotechnology can be used; it's going to be as important as electronics or the machine industry.

Obviously, we can't compete with the Japanese in manufacturing TV sets or cars, and we can't compete with the United States in turning out products of the machine industry or in building planes, but, in the fields I'm talking about, we can compete successfully with those developed countries, because we have established cooperation among all of our scientific research centers — something you can't do with science organized through private companies.

In capitalism, all of the scientific research centers are at war with one another — in our country, all of our scientific research centers cooperate with one another. In capitalism, all of the hospitals are competing and at war with one another, and the same is true of the doctors — in our country, all of the hospitals do research in one way or another, and all of them work closely together. Our doctors and scientists all cooperate with one another. Thus, we have exceptional conditions for giving a great boost to science. Naturally, we give priority to everything that offers us immediate benefits, that solves pressing problems in all these fields. We don't do research concerning space flights, aeronautics or the petrochemical industry; none of that would make sense for us. I can give you a lot of examples. We do research concerning everything that reduces fuel consumption; that replaces certain materials we have to import; or that offers our economy or our society rapid, immediate benefits of importance to save lives, preserve health, improve health, promote our food programs or boost our social programs — everything that will benefit our people and our economy.

Tomás Borge: How many scientific research centers does Cuba have right now?

Fidel Castro: More than 170 scientific research centers or units. No other Third World country has the level of scientific development that Cuba has already achieved. Many developed countries don't have the level of scientific development that Cuba has in many fields.

We're doing research in the field of medical equipment that uses state-of-the-art technology and we have developed and are continuing to develop lots of equipment that is very valuable — first to meet our needs and then to meet the needs of other countries and peoples.

We aren't working in electronics, in the production of components. We aren't working on the production of computers to compete with Japan and the United States, but we use electronic components and computers to develop specific pieces of equipment for a certain purpose, such as health. We're making tremendous progress with a lot of that equipment and we have designed some very important things, such as the ultramicro-analytical system, which is a combination of physical, chemical and biological elements.

This must become one of our country's pillars of development.

One day it may become more important and bring us more income than our sugar industry. It has unlimited prospects. Medicine is being developed, too.

Tomás Borge: As I understand it, Cuba also provides medical services for people from other countries who request them.
Fidel Castro: The demand of foreigners wanting medical services in Cuba is tremendous. It's so great that we can't meet it; whenever we create a new installation, the demand is greater than the capacity within a few months. This program has proved a tremendous success. In some fields, we're very advanced because of the human talent employed.

Tomás Borge: How many doctors does Cuba have now?
Fidel Castro: At the time of the triumph of the Revolution, we had 6,000 doctors — right now, we have 42,000 and in July we'll have 46,000. We have more than 20,000 medical students in our universities; thousands more go into medicine each year. Who can compete with us in the sphere of medicine? Moreover, medicine in Cuba is also social; it isn't based on private interests, on money-grubbing, and its quality is growing precisely because it has very human-oriented goals. We've already reduced our infant mortality to extremely low levels; it was even reduced in 1991, in the special period.

Tomás Borge: What is Cuba's infant mortality rate now?
Fidel Castro: Right now, it's 10.7 for every thousand live births, but we're struggling, even in the special period, to bring it down to under 10. What a feat! Figure it out for yourself: we've saved tens of thousands of lives by reducing our infant mortality to that level.

Tomás Borge: Isn't the cost of reducing the rate farther too great?
Fidel Castro: Of course, it's expensive; it's more sophisticated. Bringing our infant mortality rate down from 20 cost a great deal. Economically speaking, it's relatively easy to bring it down to 20, but can you resign yourself to 20? If you have it at 20 and don't struggle to reduce it to 10, you'll be resigning yourself — in the

case of Cuba — to having 1,700 babies die each year. Can you resign yourself to having 1,700 babies die in a year?

When we get it down to 10 and can reduce it to 7, we must struggle to get it down to 7, because that means saving the lives of hundreds of babies a year. In this case, we'll be saving the lives of nearly 520 babies if we manage to reduce the infant mortality rate from 10 to 7. We'll be helping over 1,000 parents (because every child has two parents), plus all the grandparents, uncles and aunts; we'll be making those relatives happy. These are real human rights.

How can people speak of human rights in a system in which tens of thousands of children die every year?

How many children who could be saved die every year in Latin America? Around 800,000. Is a system that doesn't save them humane? The Director-General of UNICEF told me that, if the rest of Latin America had health programs like Cuba's, the lives of 800,000 children would be saved. What human rights do the policies of social confrontation, neoliberalism and the International Monetary Fund offer? What human rights? What are the policies in favor of human rights in the United States? That 800,000 children should die every year? That the number of children who die should even increase? What does that have to do with democracy, human rights and the happiness and well-being of human beings? All of the demagogy and politicking that surrounds this is repulsive, because men, women and children are being starved to death, robbed of dozens of years of life, of well-being and of everything with those pitiless systems. How can they keep on talking about human rights? For me, democracy is what we have, and human rights are what we're implementing.

I could go on talking for a long time about what we're doing to help people and the letters we have received from people both in Cuba and abroad — because we've helped to save the lives of many, many people outside Cuba, too.

Tomás Borge: I know this, Fidel, especially because of my own country, because tens of thousands of Nicaraguans have come here over the years for medical treatment.

Your familiarity with the figures on biotechnology and other aspects is impressive; you keep close tabs on all this. People even say that you've made your main assistant — José Miyar, "Chomy", who, I understand, is a doctor — responsible for giving priority to those programs.

Fidel Castro: A lot of people are working on this. I asked Chomy to train somebody to do 80 percent of the work he's doing now — he's Secretary of the Council of State — so he can dedicate 80 percent of his time to the program for developing biotechnology, the one I mentioned, promoting coordination and boosting that activity. He's one of the people who represent me in all those institutions, even though I also have a lot of personal contact with them — I'm in contact with one scientific institution or another almost every day. This is part of my work, the part I like best.

Tomás Borge: Don't the difficulties of daily life upset the people?

Fidel Castro: The difficulties are great, and people are only human. They suffer if they want to have things they can't have, if they want more and can't have it. But human beings also have the ability to understand — they're intelligent, and we keep on explaining what's being done and how, so the people give us tremendous cooperation. They know that our cause is just and that we must defend it. Our people know that they bear a great historic responsibility and they know that they're carrying out quite a feat. This stimulates them.

I am amazed by the Cuban people and love them more and more as time goes by because of how they are responding. I see their good qualities multiplying. The people are growing in stature in these circumstances and are carrying out tremendous feats. This isn't anything new for me, though — we waged the war and the Revolution with the people. With the people, we carried out internationalist missions and built socialism.

I mentioned the war of liberation, Tomás; it was extremely difficult. When we began the struggle, we didn't have any weapons. We started from scratch, pitting ourselves against an organized army with a tradition and a body of officers trained in military academies and advised and supplied by the United States. War is the best place in which you can appreciate the qualities of human beings, especially in the mountains.

As Martí said, climbing mountains makes humans into brothers and sisters. Climbing mountains also enables people to express themselves and show what they are: their capacity to make sacrifices and do hard work. I've known people who preferred death to work in the mountains.

I've seen the virtues of the human spirit in the farmers and workers — who, basically, were the ones who joined our liberation army. I've had many experiences related to people's good qualities, and human beings are the most marvelous thing there is.

We may suffer, but the people will keep on helping one another, struggling and fighting. They won't get demoralized or discouraged and they will feel proud of what they're doing.

Naturally, I'm not going to say that everybody will have the same reaction — I'm taking about the majority, the vast majority. Every society has its weak parts, its weak people, people who aren't as willing to make sacrifices, people who aren't stimulated as much by great causes, people with less awareness. We have them, too. On the one hand, this implies erosion; on the other, it implies strength. Some people grow weak and are demoralized. Others grow stronger; their morale increases, and they grow with it. These are two phenomena which can be observed side by side in circumstances such as these.

CHAPTER 11

Human rights in Cuba

The banner of human rights waved by Carter's pious hands was crumpled by his successors. Those gentlemen were partial and astute when there was talk of repression in El Salvador, Guatemala and Chile — in any case, they absolved those governments — and they didn't have any scruples in their incisive, fanciful references to Cuba and Nicaragua.

The Reagan and Bush Administrations bored everyone to tears with human rights, and, apart from their messianism and the barefaced malice of the Santa Fe documents, have dedicated themselves to crowing about democracy.

They — and others less famous but just as presumptuous — are spending all their free time dreaming up new arguments to persuade us that human rights have been violated in Cuba and that the Cuban people are screeching liked a deflowered maiden, calling on everyone to put an end to their calvary.

Seldom have I heard Fidel Castro present such solid and eloquent reasoning concerning respect for human rights in Cuba as on one of these three memorable nights.

However, I think that the Cuban leader forgot some elements, including the fact that education in his country is free of charge at all levels and that education is compulsory in Cuba though the ninth grade — with Cuba the only country in the world to have achieved these two educational feats.

T.B.

Tomás Borge: People in Latin America and other geographic areas speak insistently of alleged human rights violations in Cuba. What is the real situation of human rights in your country?

Fidel Castro: What do I think about the question of human rights? Speaking calmly and objectively, I am thoroughly convinced that no country in the world has done more than Cuba to protect human rights.

No children in Cuba have to beg or are homeless; no children have to scrounge for a living in the streets. In the rest of the world — including the developed countries, but mainly in the other Third World countries — tens of millions of homeless children who have no parents or support of any kind are begging in the streets, swallowing fire and doing other spectacular things to make a living. In view of this, I ask you: is there any country that has done more than we have to protect human rights?

Look at the numbers of sick children who don't receive any medical attention and the numbers of children who are illiterate, even in the developed capitalist countries. In our country, everyone knows how to read and write. Hundreds of millions of children in the world don't have access to medical treatment, but in Cuba every child has a school to go to and has access to medical care. Has any country done more for human rights in this regard than we have?

In other parts of the world, children are bought and sold and even exported to other countries; companies have been created for exporting children. In some cases, quite frequently, children are even sold so their vital organs can be used for transplants. That has never happened in our country. With regard to this aspect, has any country done more than Cuba to protect human rights?

Think of child prostitution, which is quite generalized in the rest of the Third World, with children even used for scenes in pornographic films and tableaux. There isn't any child prostitution in Cuba, none at all. Has any country done more for human rights in this regard than we have?

Many countries have infant mortality rates of more than 100 for every thousand live births, and the average in Latin America is over 60. This means that hundreds of thousands of children die each year. However, Cuba — a Third World, underdeveloped country that is now facing a double blockade — has brought down its infant mortality rate for children under a year old to 10.7 and the figures for 1 to 5-year-olds and 5 to 15-year-olds to practically nothing. In the more than 30 years since the triumph of the Revolution, the lives of hundreds of thousands of children have been saved in Cuba. As regards this aspect, has any country done more than Cuba to protect human rights?

In Cuba, every human being has a truly equal opportunity to develop physically and intellectually, without any discrimination based on sex or race. This holds true for everyone, without any differences between rich and poor. Has any country done more for human rights in this regard than we have?

So far, I've spoken only about children.

In many countries, there are millions of beggars, women who have been forced into prostitution and adolescents and citizens in general who take drugs — a commonplace situation in the developed capitalist world and in the rest of the Third World. In contrast, Cuba doesn't have any beggars, women have no need to become prostitutes and there aren't any drugs. All this is the result of the Revolution's humanitarian work of giving everybody opportunities, creating the conditions for eliminating prostitution and the traffic in drugs and providing a healthy environment. In this regard, has any country done more than Cuba to protect human rights?

Life expectancy has increased considerably — to over 75 years — since the triumph of the Revolution. We have given every citizen dozens of additional years and the possibility of having a healthier, safer life. In other countries, life expectancy is 40, 45, 50 or 55 years. As regards this aspect, has any country done more than Cuba for human rights?

The world in general, but especially the Third World, is full of people who are unemployed, young people who are out of work and old people who don't have any social protection. In our country, everybody — men and women, alike — has been given the possibility of working, and all citizens have social protection through retirement, pensions and social security. No one has been left to their fate in all the years of the Revolution. Has any country done more in this regard than Cuba to protect human rights?

Discrimination against women — which is so strongly entrenched in all other parts of the world, including the other Third World countries — has disappeared in Cuba. In fact, women constitute nearly 60 percent of the country's technical work force and are paid the same wages as men, with no wage discrimination — a form of discrimination that is an everyday phenomenon in the rest of the world. It doesn't exist in Cuba, where women have been liberated and have job opportunities, protection, education, health care and nursery schools for their children. Has any country done more for human rights in this regard than Cuba?

Take racial discrimination. The Revolution wiped it out in this country. Now, all citizens have full equality, including equal opportunities without any racial discrimination — a fact that nobody can dispute in our country. Few other countries in the world can say the same. Has any country really done more for human rights in this regard than Cuba?

Look at the effect that equality — equal opportunities and equal treatment — has on human beings and their happiness. Those irritating differences between millionaires and beggars have disappeared; no one has to beg here now. People need more than bread: they need honor, dignity, respect and to be treated like human beings. In this regard, has any country done more than Cuba to protect human rights?

All over the world, in capitalist society, including the capitalist Third World countries, some citizens have been alienated and are considered worthless. They are taken to vote for somebody every four, five or six years without even knowing who they're voting for or why — because, often, their low political cultural level and low cultural level in general don't give them a chance to decide freely. They're influenced by all the mechanisms for exerting mental and psychological influence in decision-making — and then nobody cares about them any more. There isn't any sense of identification between such people and the state, the government and the society in which they live. They are condemned to a desperate struggle for survival without any social worth, respect or consideration. In a country such as ours, the situation is entirely different, with total identification and full participation by citizens in all activities — political activities, activities in defense of our country, cultural activities and activities for developing the country. Has any country done more for human rights in this regard than Cuba?

For more than 30 years, no measures of force have been employed against the people. For more than 30 years, no workers', farmers', students' or other people's demonstrations have been repressed. For more than 30 years, no police or soldiers have hurled themselves against the people in order to beat them up or repress them, and no fire trucks, tear gas or buckshot — which are everyday things in the developed capitalist countries and in other Third World countries — have been used against the people here. Has any country demonstrated more respect for human rights than Cuba?

With the Revolution and with socialism, we have created a sense of solidarity and fraternity. In this regard, has any country done more for human rights than Cuba?

We have experiences and live in an atmosphere unlike those in any other country in the world. Here, we share what we have. We don't have any gross inequality, with some having much more than they need and dying of heart attacks and cholesterol, while others starve to death. Here, we share everything — our country belongs to all of us, and its riches belong to all of us, too. Has any country done more for its people than Cuba?

Here, our citizens feel that they count; they are a part of society; they feel they have a national dignity and a homeland — something that is very rare and inaccessible to the vast majority of the people in today's world. Has any country done more for human rights in this regard than Cuba?

I'm talking about the things that, in my opinion, constitute true humanitarianism, the policy of promoting the dignity of human beings and their well-being. Inequality causes terrible suffering, which is unknown to our people.

Tomás Borge: Even so, Fidel, people say that many abuses have been committed in Cuba. Every day, in the mass media, I hear and see references to those supposed human rights violations...

Fidel Castro: Cuba has been grossly slandered. Its enemies have even spoken of physical violence against people, torture and such things. They have written and multiplied all that calumny against Cuba. You shouldn't be asking me about this — you should be asking the people what the facts are.

Our Revolution has a characteristic — and I say this without wishing to offend or hurt anybody — that very few revolutions have had in all of history: our people have been taught to hate crime, to hate torture, to hate the use of physical violence against individuals, to hate abuses of power. This is what inspires us in our struggle, what mobilizes us and unites us: our frontal attack on all those forms of injustice. We have employed this approach consistently throughout our war of liberation and our revolutionary history.

I wonder if there has ever been another war in which no prisoners were ever struck, tortured or murdered, any other war in which physical means were never used to compel prisoners to make a statement. I wonder if there has ever been another war like that. In our 25-month-long war of liberation, there were no cases of violations of this kind — not one. We even set all of our prisoners free.

Why did we win the war? Because we had a humanitarian policy. We won people over with that policy. It may seem idealistic, because there's always a justification for doing cruel things in times of danger in a war.

The people were trained in this, but the most interesting thing is that, for the past 33 years, ever since the triumph of the Revolution, those norms established in our Rebel Army have been maintained. I can state categorically — all the people know this — that, since the triumph of the Revolution, nobody has been assassinated, no prisoners have been tortured and no physical violence has been used against prisoners. How many other countries, revolutions, states that have had civil wars or states that have participated in foreign wars can say the same? But we have every right to.

What is behind that determination to stain the clean history of the Revolution, which has set an unprecedented example, if not the imperialists' aim of slandering the Revolution, undermining its moral authority and destroying it? The people who make these attacks know it's all a lie; the imperialists know this very well, indeed, because they know what our norms are.

In Latin America, we know of countless cases of violence, torture, disappearances, death squads and other crimes. Death squad killings are everyday things in many Latin American countries. In the 33 years since the triumph of the Revolution, Cuba hasn't had any death squads or any victims of those illegal methods of imposing order. No people have disappeared in Cuba in the last 33 years. None of those phenomena that occur all the time in other parts of the world have occurred in Cuba since the triumph of the Revolution. I think we are setting an exceptional example in this.

These are the facts, the objective facts. Don't the people know what's going on? How could the people be unaware of it if somebody were to disappear or be tortured in this country? I consider this an affront to our people, who have been educated in the principles of respect for human beings and in the struggle to promote human welfare. I think it is an affront to our people to suppose that they would support a revolution that didn't have such a blameless record or that were unable to denounce any violation of that kind that might be committed in our country, because our people wouldn't accept — wouldn't tolerate — any such thing.

I warn you: the Cuban people are radical. As a rule, they want strong measures, strong demands, strong punishments — not the opposite. Often, the people have criticized the Revolution because it hasn't been tougher or more demanding. The Revolution has never been criticized for having been excessively harsh in the struggle, in its measures against the counterrevolution. All criticism has been because it hasn't been tough enough, because the masses always tend to be more demanding and use more rigorous measures. If we've had any problems with public opinion in Cuba, it's for lack — not excess — of tough measures.

The lies about this are told outside our country, are repeated all over and confuse many people, deceive lots of people, because there's an art, a science, for engaging in this kind of propaganda. But, in Cuba, has anyone — who isn't a counterrevolutionary, a

CIA agent, an individual who serves imperialism's aim of destroying the Revolution — made any charge of this nature? Could it be that the people are unaware of a different policy that has been implemented in our country?

This is why, Tomás, I think we're an exceptional case as regards human rights. No other country has done what we have.

We have applied that policy not only here but also on the internationalist missions in which we've participated. Our soldiers took all of those habits and norms that guided our conduct in the mountains with them when they went to Angola, Ethiopia or wherever else they were, and those norms also governed our conduct in the cooperation we gave the revolutionary movement. Never can it honestly be said that a Cuban soldier on an internationalist mission murdered or tortured a prisoner. Our soldiers never did that.

Moreover, we provided health care and schools for our people, and tens of thousands of Cuban workers have helped to save lives. They have saved hundreds of thousands of lives in other countries. Not only have we done humanitarian work in our own country, but we've offered our cooperation to help other peoples. No other people in the present era has carried out more internationalist missions of this kind than Cuba. More than 10,000 Cuban doctors have fulfilled internationalist missions. How many lives have they saved in the course of more than 20 years?

Thousands of Cuban teachers have taught children in other parts of the world. What other country has done that? What country had more crusaders, more missionaries practicing human solidarity, not only with its own people but also with others?

Has any government or country done more for human rights in this regard than Cuba? What basis can there be for all the slander campaigns they launch against our country? Naturally, we're accustomed to this, and it just rolls off our backs, because we're used to the imperialists' baseness. How can they survive if not with propaganda? How would they survive without lies? How can they explain all of the crimes they commit against the world, if not with lies and calumny, trying to discredit those who oppose them?

I am sure that the masses and the peoples will obey their

instincts and not be swayed by the volume and intensity of that campaign the imperialists are waging against Cuba.

Look what happens in the United Nations, where Cuba's role is recognized — not publicly, but whenever there's a secret ballot. Cuba gets a majority of the votes. Many countries there vote for us when it's a secret ballot. When the vote is public, it's a different matter, because conflicts arise: problems for their economic interests, because of the reprisals the United States will take against them.

People acknowledge what Cuba is, its policy of solidarity, its internationalist policy, its humanitarian policy. Now, not only do the peoples have a great instinct for discovering and recognizing the truth, but the representatives of the governments acknowledge what Cuba has done.

Meanwhile, we aren't going to be demoralized or discouraged by this kind of campaign; we aren't going to change. We're going to keep on applying the same policy and maintain our system of equality. What's important to us is having a clear conscience and the support of public opinion in our own country, Tomás.

Tomás Borge: Many people — some of them, I think, in good faith — think it would have been better if Cuba hadn't applied the most severe penalties against enemies of the Revolution who engaged in illegal activities. Even though not all of them in the latest known case were shot, at least one of them was. I'd like to hear your comments...

Fidel Castro: For one thing, that's related to another topic: to the death penalty — whether or not the death penalty should exist for crimes, whether or not it should be removed from all the statutes.

I don't think anybody likes the death penalty, and many people — including friends of Cuba — have contacted us expressing their point of view, not for political motives. Some good, honest people did this. We also have to distinguish between the honest people — of whom there are many — and the dishonest people who organized the campaigns about all these things. That's why some honest people didn't agree with the measures we took.

The death penalty has been applied under long-standing laws, for only extremely serious crimes. We must defend ourselves. What weapons do we use? The weapons of legality, of laws, of the courts against crime. We use them to defend our society.

There are common crimes and counterrevolutionary crimes. Often, counterrevolutionary crimes are even more loathsome than common ones. How can we defend ourselves if we don't avail ourselves of the law — do we set up death squads, make people disappear and resort to such methods? We'll never do that. We don't have any means for defending the Revolution other than the laws and courts of justice.

Now, if everybody were to agree to do away with the death penalty, we could eliminate it entirely, but we can't do this unilaterally when we're continually threatened by the United States, involved in a struggle for survival, in a life-or-death situation. We can't disarm unilaterally and renounce the application of severe penalties for cases in which serious crimes are committed against our people — especially in a situation in which the counterrevolutionaries are being told and taught to believe that the Revolution is about to collapse, that the Revolution won't last long, and that, at most, they'll get a few months in jail, and they aren't running any risks.

In the case of those men who came from Miami armed with dynamite and with plans for carrying out acts of terrorism in public meetings and other places that could cost the lives of five, 10, 30 or 40 people, our basic sense of duty to our people, to our citizens — men, women and children who could be the victims of those acts of terrorism planned by individuals who invaded our country, who entered our country and committed an extremely serious crime — makes it impossible for us to cede to pressure, to the concerns even of our friends or to the negative effects of the campaigns launched to urge us to grant clemency. What justification could the Council of State have had for granting clemency to those sentenced by our courts of justice?

Three of them came, and the courts investigated and analyzed what they had done. Our courts were generous; they gave the maximum sentence only to the one primarily responsible, who was most aware of the seriousness of what they were doing. Who was he? A common criminal — not what we call a counter-revolutionary criminal — who had gone to the United States illegally, was recruited there and prepared to come here to carry out acts of terrorism.

If the government had granted clemency, what would we have achieved? It would have promoted this kind of adventure, and, in a few months, there would be not one expedition but 10, manned by people who had been deceived and led to believe that the Revolution was on its last legs and who came here to kill people so they would later on receive awards, acclaim and other fruits of their betrayal and crimes. What could we say to the people if we had granted clemency? What could we say to our fellow citizens about this, and what could we say to them when another crime of this nature took place?

We didn't have any moral reason, any justification, for granting clemency, except for being swayed by considerations that had nothing to do with protecting our people's lives and safety. Individuals who try to do such things in our country and commit such crimes against innocent people shouldn't think that, when they do such things, the Council of State will grant them clemency or make the mistake of divorcing itself from the people out of weakness or failure to do its duty.

A few days later, the crimes at the Tarará water sports base took place. I don't want to go into it, because it would take too long, but I witnessed a 23-year-old's agony for 35 days. They say that Christ was on the cross for a few hours; I saw a young man crucified for 35 days, with an epic battle waged to save his life. He was the only one who survived — for 35 days — a quadruple murder perpetrated by common criminals urged on by the United States. When criminals arrive there after committing such crimes, they are welcomed with open arms and hailed as heroes.

The indignation which that attack aroused in the people was tremendous and the courts sentenced the guilty parties. Their victims had been murdered after being tied up; they were slaughtered. Why should we have granted clemency?

As for the death penalty, the country in which the most people are given the death penalty is the United States. The U.S. record is horrible. Should we believe that all of them are common criminals? What about all the people who are unemployed, without any support, and have to commit crimes in order to survive? Isn't there any political responsibility?

Were all those who have been sent to the electric chair in the United States — or to the gas chamber or who have been given lethal injections — were all of them common criminals? No distinctions are made there between common criminals and political prisoners. Many prisoners in the United States were forced into crime by causes that are directly linked to that country's economic and social policy.

How amazing that, in the United States, the death penalty is applied mainly against Blacks and immigrants. Rarely is a white condemned to death in the United States. Nearly every day, reports come in from the United States about executions in that country. Why, then, was such an enormous campaign launched against Cuba, simply because we didn't grant clemency to those individuals who committed loathsome crimes? Why should we have to disarm and grant clemency to such people? I assure you that the Council of State's attitude was correct and it will have the same attitude in any similar circumstances, because we have a very clear sense of our duties and responsibilities.

Tomás Borge: Many people think that there is sexual discrimination in Cuba. What are your views on homosexuality, lesbianism and free love?
Fidel Castro: Well, Tomás, you're asking me questions that are more appropriate for the confessional. You're acting like a priest, not a journalist, asking me what I think about such things, but I won't refuse to answer.

You spoke about sexual discrimination. I already told you that we have eradicated sexual discrimination. More precisely, we have done the most any government can do to put an end to discrimination against women.

It has been a long struggle and it has been successful and achieved great results in ending discrimination against women, but I can't say that such discrimination has been entirely eradicated. We still have some male chauvinists; I think that there is much less male chauvinism here than in any other Latin

American country, but it still exists. It has been a part of our people's character for centuries and had many causes, running from the Arab influence in Spain to other influences by the Spaniards themselves, because we inherited male chauvinism — and many other bad habits — from the conquistadores.

That was an historical legacy — stronger in some countries than in others — but in no country have the people fought harder against male chauvinism than in ours, and I don't think that any country has achieved greater tangible and practical results in this struggle than Cuba. We have made a real advance — we can see it, especially in the young people, but we can't say that sexual discrimination has been completely wiped out and we mustn't lower our guard. We must continue struggling in this regard, because male chauvinism is an historical, ancestral legacy. We've struggled hard against it, made progress and obtained results, but we must keep on struggling.

I'm not going to deny that, at one point, male chauvinism also influenced our attitude toward homosexuality. I, myself — you're asking me for my own opinion — don't have any phobia against homosexuals. I've never felt that phobia and I've never promoted or supported policies against homosexuals. I would say that it corresponded to a given stage and is largely associated with that legacy of male chauvinism. I try to have a more humane, scientific approach to the problem. Often, it becomes a tragedy, because of what the parents think — some parents whose son is homosexual turn it into a tragedy. It's really too bad they react this way and make it a tragedy for the individual, as well.

I don't consider homosexuality to be a phenomenon of degeneration. I've always had a more rational approach, considering it to be one of the natural aspects and tendencies of human beings which should be respected. That's how I view it. I think there should be consideration for a family in this situation. It would be good if the families themselves had another mentality, another approach, when a circumstance of this nature occurs. I am absolutely opposed to any form of repression, contempt, scorn or discrimination with regard to homosexuals. That's what I think.

Tomás Borge: Can a homosexual be a member of the Communist Party?

Fidel Castro: There has been a lot of prejudice concerning all this — that's a fact. But we've concentrated our struggle against prejudices of another kind.

For example, men's and women's conduct was judged by different standards. We had that for years in the Party, and I waged battles and argued a lot about it. If a man was unfaithful, it didn't constitute a problem or a worry, but, if a woman was unfaithful, that became the subject of discussion in the Party nucleus. There was a double standard, for judging the sexual relations of men and women. I had to fight hard, very hard, against those deep-rooted prejudices. There wasn't any doctrine or education in this regard; instead, there were many male chauvinist concepts and prejudices in our society.

I haven't answered your question about free love. I don't know exactly what you mean by free love, but, interpreting it as the freedom to love, I don't have any objection to it.

Tomás Borge: What about believers, Fidel?

Fidel Castro: We've had to struggle against many forms of discrimination.

We had to tackle the problem of discrimination against religious believers, and it wasn't easy to win that battle in the Party — especially with the young people — and get them to understand that it wasn't fair to use religious beliefs as a reason for refusing to allow people who had all the required revolutionary and patriotic virtues to join the Communist Party.

CHAPTER 12

Loyalty to principles

Cuba is an island country with tall palm trees and impassioned poets, a land of hurricanes and mysteries with unforeseeable responses. The first time I visited it, in December 1960, it was brimming with revolutionary watchwords and power struggles.

Early on, an insuperable contradiction arose between Fidel and President Manuel Urrutia, a magistrate with a good record who never managed to go beyond his ideological liberalism at a time when traditional concepts had as much to do with Cuban reality as a fish with the desert sand.

Later on, a sector of the Popular Socialist Party headed by Stalinist Aníbal Escalante tried to remove the July 26 Movement and Fidel himself from the scene — an irrational thing to attempt.

Fidel always solved internal disputes by appealing for the people's support. For example, the differences with the March 13 Revolutionary Directorate, an organization parallel to the July 26 Movement, were solved with a history-making embrace.

The battle with the United States had its hottest moments at the Bay of Pigs and with the October Missile Crisis.

From a distance, I saw Fidel Castro torn with grief when Camilo Cienfuegos, the happiest and perhaps the most daring of the commanders from the Sierra Maestra, was lost in a storm while flying from Camagüey to Havana.

We were victims of the calamity that hit the national liberation movements hard when Che Guevara was murdered. Together with Carlos Fonseca, leader of the Sandinista Revolution, I listened to Fidel's grief-filled oration for the legendary combatant and his exhortation not to give in to pessimism.

Fidel also engaged in unusual public self-criticism, the most outstanding example of which, I think, was for the failure to produce 10 million metric tons of sugar in the 1970 sugarcane harvest.

Fidel has had sharp contradictions and painful losses, but he has also had beloved comrades and very close friends: Che, his brother Raúl and Celia Sánchez. Generous with recognition and affection for those who deserve them, he is uncompromising in his identification with certain norms and principles.

T. B.

Tomás Borge: Raúl Castro is not only your beloved brother but also, perhaps, your main colleague.

Fidel Castro: Raúl is a person with exceptional qualities. I don't know how much he has been harmed by being my brother, because, when there is a tall tree, it always casts a little shade on the others. Many men have been outstanding in this country together with me: Che, Camilo, Juan Almeida and many other comrades. But, logically, a taller tree always casts a little shade.

Nobody knows what Raúl Castro could have done if he'd had the responsibility I've had. Right from the beginning, he was very serious, responsible, dedicated, committed and brave. He's demonstrated those qualities from the moment of the attack on the Moncada Garrison. Raúl wasn't involved in organizing the attack, but he took part in it.

He was very young — I was 26, so he must have been 21. It was in July, and I don't know if he had just turned 22.

He was sent with some others to an important, very strategic position — the Santiago de Cuba Court. They got there, seized the Court, disarmed the guards and took their rifles; it was a dominating position. Things didn't turn out according to plan, however. (I've explained what happened at Moncada in *History will absolve me*.) An Army patrol managed to enter the building while they were evacuating it and took them prisoner. Demonstrating the quick thinking of a tiger, Raúl seized the pistol of the sergeant who had him prisoner and took the soldiers prisoner.

Thanks to that, they escaped from what at that time would have been certain death preceded by terrible torture. In the end, he didn't escape completely and was recaptured in a town called San Luis. He was brought back and imprisoned and from then on played an important role in the trial, developing as a cadre with the other prisoners. We went through some very difficult situations — the Boniato prison, the prison on the Isle of Pines — and he was outstanding for his seriousness, sense of responsibility, quick thinking and revolutionary spirit.

When Raúl and I attacked the Moncada Garrison, we were Marxists. I had introduced him to Marxist-Leninist ideas. He was much younger than I. He was at Birán when I was a student because he had dropped out of school, but I encouraged him to keep on studying, and he was a university student when we attacked the Moncada Garrison. He was outstanding throughout that period.

Then we got out of prison. We had already thought of going to Mexico. Raúl was one of the first people we sent there — for reasons of security. Our opponents were trying to implicate us in terrorist acts. In fact, we weren't engaging in any violent activities — only political action, denouncing crimes and things of that nature. Raúl was outstanding throughout that period of organizing the *Granma* expedition in Mexico which he joined as head of a platoon with the rank of captain.

Tomás Borge: Then you demoted him to lieutenant because, at one time when he should have remained silent, he spoke out loud, something like that... Don't you remember?
Fidel Castro: No, I don't remember that. He, Almeida and Smith Comas were the three captains in the detachment. Smith Comas was a very good, very determined fellow from Cárdenas. Naturally, when you organize a detachment, excellent people immediately begin to appear; outstanding people began to appear right from the start in the groups that came on the *Granma*.

When we were scattered, Raúl stayed with a group of four or five other men and they did everything necessary to evade the enemy encirclement — the same things I did — and the only two groups that got out with weapons were Raúl's, with five weapons, and mine, with two.

I brought my rifle and another comrade brought his and there was one comrade who didn't have a weapon. My group had two rifles: one with 30 bullets and mine with around 90 bullets — my rifle with a telescopic sight, that I had nearly to the end of the war, had plenty of ammunition. Raúl came with his group and five rifles, so we had seven rifles in all. The farmers — who were religious — helped other comrades to evade the encirclement on the condition that they would hide their weapons and go back for them later. They took them to the Sierra, but without any weapons. Some of those weapons were lost.

He went through all the most difficult moments of the war and he became ever more outstanding. In the first half of 1958, I sent him to open up the Second Front — the first one was in the Sierra Maestra. I sent Almeida toward Santiago de Cuba and Raúl to an area that was farther away. With a force of around 50 or 55 men, all good soldiers — veterans — he began the march eastward through the Sierra Maestra mountains to the Second Front. He had to cross the plains, and that was the first time we had done so.

Tomás Borge: Was that where Raúl distinguished himself as a great organizer?
Fidel Castro: He was assigned a very strategic territory and he did a tremendous job there. He was quite outstanding as an organizer. He organized the struggle in that territory, increased his forces and scored a series of successes. Batista had created some groups of irregular troops there to occupy the terrain and he had sent in some paramilitary groups that pretended they were revolutionaries. Raúl established order and developed the Second Front. It grew to great size and had a lot of power. Some very important battles were waged there following the April 1958 attempt to call a general strike and also in the latter half of that year, on the eve of the final offensive.

Raúl was the first commander who opened a front outside the Sierra Maestra, and he demonstrated notable abilities as a leader and organizer, with a great sense of responsibility and considerable revolutionary firmness. He did a great political job among the farmers and had a very positive influence on all the cadres and leaders. His merits and his position in the Revolution have nothing to do with family ties. He was outstanding, like Camilo, Che, Almeida and many others, for his tremendous merits — not because we're relatives. That is the case of Raúl. His rise in rank and his role in the Revolution have nothing to do with our family ties.

After the triumph of the Revolution, he was assigned important functions. It seemed to me that he had all the qualities needed for being minister of the Revolutionary Armed Forces, and he took that post, where he has done a tremendous job of a political and educational nature, training cadres. I really think that his work is exceptionally good. That's my objective, impartial opinion.

You asked if we had any problems. Well, the fronts had a lot of autonomy for making decisions, and one time he and his men became very angry about the bombs being dropped by Batista's planes which had been supplied by the Guantánamo Naval Base. Some U.S. citizens were up there — I don't remember why — and Raúl captured them and took them prisoner. I didn't think it was a good idea to have taken that action against U.S. citizens, so I ordered him to set them free. It was an ordinary kind of order, a mission I assigned him, and he carried it out immediately. In all our lives — as far as I can recall, Tomás, but it's very unlikely I wouldn't remember — we've never had an argument. He has never raised his voice and I have never ordered him to lower his voice or punished him.

Tomás Borge: No, I didn't mean he raised his voice against you — you were supposed to keep quiet and he spoke in a normal tone of voice. I read that once.
Fidel Castro: During the war? It may be; that was normal.

Tomás Borge: At the beginning...
Fidel Castro: He was very disciplined, very careful, though. Somebody may have made a mistake and spoken normally and I told him to be quiet, something like that. Our relations have always been very fraternal and respectful, and we have never had

any kind of problem. Raúl has his own criteria, opinions, personality and character; he's very different from the Raúl portrayed in enemy propaganda. Everybody who knows him well is aware of his humanity, his great merit and his sensitivity. They are surprised when they see that Raúl, who is very friendly and affectionate, is painted as bellicose, aggressive and harsh. He has been a great teacher; I think the Ministry of the Revolutionary Armed Forces has been the best school for training cadres that we've had, always with great rigor and exigency.

Tomás Borge: I don't think that family ties have anything to do with his functions, though they are involved with the sensitivity I know Raúl has. He is a very sensitive man who is easily moved by tenderness and noble causes — I have seen that.
Fidel Castro: I've always thought that, especially in those early years, when plans were being made every day to assassinate me. It was a real possibility that one of them would succeed, so I said, "From now on, we must think of who can exercise my functions." And, really, I thought that, of all the cadres, the person who could exercise those functions best, the most respected person who could carry out those functions, was Raúl, and I stated this publicly, because that was a necessity at that time.

Raúl has been the second in command of the Revolution throughout the revolutionary period. He hasn't been more noticeable because he's been in my shadow. For people to stand out, they have to have a sphere in which they can show what they can do, where they can demonstrate their qualities.

Tomás Borge: One human being — Celia Sánchez — entered the Cuban people's hearts like a kind of shining angel. I'd like you to tell me about that exceptional woman.
Fidel Castro: As you say, Celia was an exceptional woman. I met her after the landing of the *Granma*, when we were experiencing our most difficult moments. We landed from the *Granma* on December 2, 1956. In the late afternoon on December 5, we were dealt a great setback: the enemy made a surprise attack and all our forces were scattered.

We made tactical mistakes. I had chosen a very good strategic position, but it was a rocky place, at the edge of the forest. We were exhausted and we had to walk a great distance at night. My mistake consisted of making camp not on the edge of the forest but in a small, isolated part of the woods that jutted out a bit. We grouped there, waiting from morning until late afternoon, and somebody who had served as our guide at night gave the Army our position.

The enemy used planes intensively and we remained very still, not making any movements that might be detected by the planes. They used a large number of planes that flew close to the ground, and, while we were expecting an air attack, the infantry moved up and managed to catch us unawares and scatter our detachment. It was a terrible setback.

After that, our forces began to regroup, and the work that Celia had done as leader of the July 26 Movement in the Manzanillo, Niquero and Pilón area began to bear fruit, because several farmers whom she had organized helped us in that regrouping process.

Naturally, we reorganized a little. I had two men with me; other groups had seven or eight men. Unfortunately, because of their inexperience, many of those groups did things, engaged in certain movements, that, because of the characteristics of the terrain, led them to fall into the hands of the enemy.

The people with more experience — the group Raúl was in, the group that Almeida and Che were in and some others of us who were experienced — and a few who were just plain lucky managed to escape and, often not even in woods but in sugarcane fields, managed to keep moving. We broke through the encirclement and finally regrouped later on.

When we gathered together, we were a small group of men with very few rifles in extremely difficult circumstances, but we remained determined to carry our efforts forward. We realized that the terrible setback had been the result of a tactical error, but we continued to be confident that our strategy, our kind of struggle and our selected terrain were correct, and we kept on.

It was then, in that very difficult period, that Celia became our guardian angel. She was the one who sent us supplies, who collected money and sent it to us. She was our contact with the rest of the Movement, and she was of great help in that regrouping process. We became a group of 15; then 30; and, still later, only 12. Don't think it was a matter of steady progress; we were scattered again at other times, especially in that period of the first battles, the most difficult ones, throughout the first half of 1957.

Celia was responsible for logistics, contacts, information — everything. She had gone underground and ran enormous risks in that clandestine struggle. She was very courageous. She was of key importance in reorganizing our army.

Later, she stayed with us for a while and then returned to the underground, until, when the enemy was getting too close, we suggested that she stay with the troops. At one point — I don't remember the exact date now — Celia joined our force and remained with us until the end of the war. Haydée Santamaría was with us, too.

After the triumph of the Revolution, Celia played just as important a role as she had during the war. She was a truly extraordinary woman, with great human qualities. She always helped all the comrades.

After the triumph of the Revolution, she was like a mother to all the men who had fought in the Sierra Maestra; she looked after all of them, helped solve their problems and did countless things for them. It would take too long to describe in detail everything she did in the period after the war. She was responsible for countless projects related to the people. She also took the time to gather together a large amount of materials for the historical archives, and she carried out all of the tasks assigned to her with great efficiency.

She died relatively young, of a terrible, painful disease. Celia was one of the people with the greatest merit, one of the most outstanding people of the Revolution.

Tomás Borge: A little while ago, you were talking about the role Raúl played in Mexico. Now that we're about to end this conversation, I'd like to ask you about your experiences in prison in Mexico and the people who helped to solve that problem.

Fidel Castro: I was arrested by accident. We were taking a lot of security measures, because we knew that Batista was planning to kidnap or murder me. His agents had contacted certain elements in Mexico to carry that out, and they had influence in some sectors. They had money, resources, everything. Knowing this, we had to take security measures and never went out with just one car, but with two cars, armed. Sometimes we would go out on foot and then take a car.

Standing on a corner, armed, the two men who were with me and I aroused the suspicions of some Federal Security Department agents. We had left the house on foot and a car was going to pick us up. It was getting dark, and we were walking along a cross street: I was in front, then Ramirito and then somebody else. We reached a corner where a building was under construction and I jumped in there because I saw that a suspicious-looking car with people in it was coming. I hid behind a column. I thought Ramirito was next to me. Then, when I started to pull out a machine-gun-pistol, I felt the barrel of a pistol against my neck. It was a security agent.

The agents were there in cars on another case when they became suspicious of us. What did they do? They used a very good tactic; they sent people out on foot who first captured the men who were behind me. When I saw the car coming, I thought it might be a kidnap attempt and sought shelter. I tried to defend myself, but it was a security agent — not Ramirito — who was behind me. He put his pistol barrel against my neck and arrested me.

The Federal Security Department was fighting smuggling, the Mafia and I don't know what else. Its agents thought at first that we were Cubans who were engaging in those activities and they arrested us on suspicion. They just stumbled on our revolutionary movement. After taking us in, they immediately went to various houses and other places capturing other people.

They didn't waste any time. I don't remember all the details of that operation now, but the security agents acted very quickly and thoroughly. If they found a piece of paper with an address or a telephone number on it, they immediately investigated it. They followed up all the clues they found in everybody's pockets. I was very unlucky; in the top pocket of my suit, they found a telephone number that Cándido González, a comrade who was going around with me, had given me. It was the number of the house that had the most weapons.

They followed up a lot of clues and found weapons and something that, although it wasn't what they were looking for, was important politically: a group of foreigners who were organizing an expedition against a government that had diplomatic relations with Mexico. When they realized that we weren't the people they were looking for but were revolutionaries engaging in that kind of activity, they set about following up all those clues and captured quite a few of us. I don't remember the exact number, but they didn't round up all of us. They didn't manage to capture Raúl. He was one of the ones who took measures and managed to escape, but they did get Che and I don't know how many other people, because they followed up every clue, no matter how insignificant.

The famous house whose telephone number they had found in my pocket wasn't raided — which is still a mystery to me — even though those people found out everything they could. But none of us said a word. The agents threatened that they were going to be tough, that they were going to force us to talk and all that kind of thing, but, in fact, they were quite respectful.

Who was mainly responsible for that? I think it was Fernando Gutiérrez Barrios. Gutiérrez Barrios was the chief of the Federal Security Department, and he behaved like a gentleman. After he realized who we were and noted our firmness, decency and convictions, the agents treated us with complete respect — though without ceasing to be rigorous in their interrogations, which went on and on. That is, they viewed the matter as a political problem, not a common crime, smuggling or anything like that. That was the way Gutiérrez Barrios treated us.

Naturally, they followed all the procedures and carried out all the investigations. They picked up everybody they could and handed us over to the Ministry of the Interior and the courts. We wound up in prison. I was in the immigration prison for quite some time — at least, it seemed like a long time to me. You could ask some of the others how many weeks it was.

We lost weapons and funds, and they found out what we

were planning to do. Up until then, we had been working with great discretion, because some of the Cubans in Mexico who weren't in our group were always making contacts and spying for Batista and the Mexican Secret Police. It was Federal Security Department agents, not the Secret Police, that picked us up. We were lucky it was the security agents and that they had a chief with Gutiérrez Barrios's personal characteristics. Gutiérrez Barrios even treated us in a respectful, gentlemanly way while we were in prison.

We lost our weapons and were found out, but that wasn't all: there was a great national and international outcry. Naturally, as a matter of course, they accused us of being communists — and it didn't help matters when, after he was picked up, Che felt it was his duty to say whatever he thought. "Are you a communist?" "Yes, I'm a communist." The security people and the judges argued with Che about communism and even Khrushchev's denunciation of Stalin. Being discovered caused us a lot of trouble, among other reasons, because a number of us were imprisoned.

In the end, they let some of our group go, leaving Che and me for last... I tell you, it was really something: Che, with the spirit of a martyr in Roman times, confessing he was a communist! He believed it was his revolutionary duty to express his ideas, but it really complicated the situation. There was a tremendous uproar about that. And, as I told you, Che argued with the judges, the police and everybody else who interrogated him. Che didn't follow the correct tactic and he complicated things. As a result, they held Che and me longer; we were the last two still in prison.

Who helped us to get out? Lázaro Cárdenas, whom I didn't know and with whom we didn't have any contact. Because of his noble spirit and his great concern for all legitimate, revolutionary causes, when he learned that we were in prison, he took an interest in having us set free and finally achieved it.

That was what the great Lázaro Cárdenas did. We went to see him later and thanked him. We will never forget him, not only because we know of what he did for Mexico and his great role in the Mexican Revolution and Mexican life but also because of what he did for us, whom he didn't even know. He did us a great service at a decisive moment.

We managed to remain in Mexico, though under surveillance. From then on, some of the expeditionaries had to go to the Ministry of the Interior every Monday to report in. We left Mexico in those and even worse conditions. We had decided on a date and everything was ready, but, the week before we were to leave, an individual deserted and turned traitor. Many people in the group didn't think he would inform on us; they thought he was disgusted by some measures that had been taken but that he wouldn't turn traitor. We couldn't do anything except try our best to get him to return, but we didn't succeed in that. He had a lot of information, including the fact that we were planning to go on the *Granma*.

We thought about leaving earlier than planned, but we were under tremendous harassment the last week we were in Mexico. As a result of that betrayal — the information was sent on to Batista — Batista presented a denunciation to the Mexican government. I was the only one who knew all of the details, however. The work had been compartmentalized, and I was the only one who knew where all the weapons were. However, it took more than one person to move and store weapons, bullets and the rest of the supplies, so a small team did that — sometimes one person, sometimes more than one. Even so, some of our weapons were seized. It was a sort of competition between us, with the security agents trying to seize our weapons and us trying to move them out before they got there.

We began to work out what effects his squealing might have: where the danger might lie. We tried to take the weapons out of those places where we thought they were in danger. We rescued a large part of them, especially the rifles with telescopic sights. We got to the places where they were in danger ahead of the Security agents — we knew which places those were — and we took them out of those houses and kept them in suitcases in motels and hotels between Mexico City and Tuxpan.

So, our departure from Mexico wasn't easy. We managed to get the weapons and men to the ship and got it ready around 24 hours before departure. We went down the Tuxpan River when storm warnings were ordering all vessels to stay in port. We had to go past the naval station at dawn. Before we got to the ocean, the water was quite calm, but, when we got to the Gulf, it was hell. I don't know how the *Granma* wasn't sunk.

That sums up the final stage, in which we got out of prison.

Tomás Borge: Several times, you referred to "Ramirito." Did you mean Ramiro Valdés?
Fidel Castro: Yes.

Tomás Borge: Is he especially close to you?
Fidel Castro: Yes, of course. I have great esteem for him.

Tomás Borge: I think he deserves it.
Fidel Castro: I know he's a good friend of yours, too.

Tomás Borge: Of all possible negative human attitudes, which is the one you hate most? And, of all the positive ones, which is the one you most value?
Fidel Castro: The one I hate most is treason, disloyalty. Loyalty and firmness of principles are among the ones I value most. I would say that the one I detest the most is betrayal of principles, and the one I most admire is loyalty to principles.

CHAPTER 13

Of books and reading

The last time I arrived in Havana, with Marcela, I took a new look at the beckoning Malecón seawall drive, the enchantment of Old Havana, and the delicious white rice, black beans and cholesterol of the Bodeguita del Medio restaurant.

We visited art galleries and museums; went to the house of the great painter Manuel Mendive; and, amazed, discovered Tomás Sánchez's blending of colors in his paintings. We bought dozens of books by Cuban authors and sailed through the sea of metaphors of the new poetry and Cuba's vast river of fiction that is largely unknown in the rest of Latin America.

The enormous runs of the past have been substantially reduced for lack of paper — which is a result of the shortage of petroleum, that is the fruit of new world geopolitics — which, in turn, is determined by the U.S. economic blockade.

The Cuban Revolution hasn't made any strategic mistakes in its cultural policy. Except for a short period at the beginning of the 1970s, when some officials tried to impose "socialist realism," there has never been an official aesthetic model. The tremendous development of artistic creation, especially in literature, is due to this and to institutional support, in which Fidel Castro himself has had a hand.

Che's opinions on this have always been kept in mind. Prophetically, he described the problems of art in a young society, such as a socialist one, which generally lacks "the knowledge and intellectual daring needed to meet the task of developing the new man with methods different from the conventional ones.... What is sought then is simplification, something everyone can understand, something functionaries understand. True artistic inquiry ends, and the problem of general

155

*culture is reduced to taking some things from the socialist present and
some from the dead (therefore, not dangerous) past. Thus socialist
realism arises upon the foundations of the art of the last century."*

T. B.

Tomás Borge: I have heard it said that you are a confirmed
reader, not only of government reports but also of literary works.
What book are you reading now, what is the last one you finished
reading, and which one are you thinking of reading next?
Fidel Castro: Throughout my life, Tomás, I've always read as
many books as I could, and it makes me sad that I don't have
more time for reading. I suffer when I see libraries and lists of
book titles of any kind, regretting that I can't spend my life
reading and studying.

I've read all kinds of literature. What I liked best of the first
things I read were books of history: the history of Cuba, world
history and many biographies. I've read almost all of the main,
classical biographies. In senior high school, I was in contact with
literature, mainly the classics of Spanish literature.

Naturally, the Bible was one of the classical works I read.
Anyone who analyzes the way I speak will find that I use biblical
terms, because I studied in religious schools for 12 years, with the
La Salle Brothers and, mainly, the Jesuits. I studied at the La Salle
Brothers school from the first to fifth grades and, from the fifth
grade through senior high school, with the Jesuits. They
concentrated on Spanish literature, not world literature. I didn't
have much contact with world literature until later on. I had a
chance to read many books. This was also true when I was in
prison. The nearly two years I was in prison, between 1953 and
1955, was the period when I had the most time for reading.

I have always been fond of Cuban history, because of what it
tells us about the people who fought for our independence —
especially Martí and his works.

Martí was the first author whose works I read most avidly. It
would be difficult to find any of Martí's political proclamations or

speeches — which fill two thick volumes, around 2,000 pages or more — that I didn't read when I was in senior high school or university. Later, I read biographies of our patriots — Máximo Gómez, Carlos Manuel de Céspedes, Ignacio Agramonte and Antonio Maceo — everything that mentioned them. How I soaked up that literature! I got my first political training by reading Cuban history as a student and after I had graduated I kept on reading. I have always liked reading, and I still like it. I'm a fanatic about any literature that describes our wars of independence and the people who fought for Cuba's independence.

Then, there's political literature. I began to dip into political literature as a university student, especially in my studies of political economy, which I began in my first year in the School of Law. It was capitalist political economy, but it included all the classics, with references to all of the main schools of economics. In my second year, I kept on studying political economy and also took up labor legislation, which was when I began to hear of people going more deeply into Marx, Engels, Lenin and the various schools, and I read a lot about all of them.

Before that, when I was studying capitalist political economy, I became a kind of utopian socialist. I made a critical assessment of all that capitalist political economy and it seemed crazy, absurd, anarchic and chaotic to me. Therefore, socialist ideas had already put down deep roots in me. Before reading Marx, Engels, Lenin and all the other classics, I had come to the conclusion, based on my own analysis of capitalist political economy, that capitalism was crazy and chaotic. I began to develop theories of how the economy ought to be organized.

The books on economics in the School of Law were many and heavy going and the exams were hard, but I got top grades in that subject, even though a very large proportion of my class flunked. I had mulled all of those things over, even though I didn't have a lot of time for studying in the first few years, because I was involved in political activities and also sports. I was an athlete and a political activist, and I also wanted to study.

Of course, as I began to develop ideas and analyze the existing economic system on my own, my spirit became fertile ground for Marxist-Leninist ideas. That was the path, the open door, by which I entered, and I became a fanatic — to give it a name — an impassioned follower of the ideas of Marx, Engels and Lenin. From then on, I read a great deal of political literature.

I have spent a lot of time reading — not only history and geography but also political literature and world literature. I'm always reading. For example, I have a huge collection of books on Bolívar; I admire him tremendously. I consider Bolívar to have been the greatest of the greats in history, a man who overcame difficulties and surmounted all obstacles, a truly extraordinary person.

I have also read a lot about Hannibal of Carthage, his expeditions, his campaigns in Italy, his wars and battles, and everything I could find about Alexander the Great, Julius Caesar, other great figures in history, and the great military leaders of more modern times, such as Napoleon.

Bolívar is my favorite among the great figures in history. And, of course, Martí. Martí was a Bolívar in the sphere of thought, and Bolívar was a genius in politics and war. He was a statesman, because he had opportunities to head states -- which Martí didn't have.

Bolívar's idea of uniting this immense region in the midst of such enormous difficulties was unprecedented, and it was in addition to his efforts to liberate all of these countries. The effort of trying to unite them was a fundamental, vital idea for all of Our America, for all our region and for all of the peoples of Iberian origin — that is, of Spanish and Portuguese origin, that mixture that began to be formed 500 years ago. Bolívar's thinking and ideas are extremely important.

But, to define Martí: I said he was a Bolívar in the sphere of thought, at the apex. I don't know if this will brand me as sectarian, but I can't recall anybody else of his intellectual caliber. Martí was a fanatic about Bolívar — his greatness and his aims. I have read many books, so I have the right to choose the historical figures with whom I have the most fellow-feeling.

It's hardly necessary to tell you that I have read many books about revolutions. I think that, over the years, I have read all the books ever written about the French Revolution, many about the

Bolshevik Revolution, countless numbers about the Mexican Revolution and also many about the Chinese Revolution. Moreover, I've paid some attention to economic writings; I've read about economic problems, though perhaps not as extensively as about historical matters.

In prison, I went about my studies systematically. We set up a school, with courses in philosophy. We read a lot of world literature. For two years, I spent between 14 and 15 hours a day reading, except for the time I spent writing manifestos, messages and letters in invisible ink: lime juice. I don't know how many things we wrote in lime juice on the ordinary letters we sent our relatives. They ironed them or put them in the oven and the invisible writing would appear. We used that procedure all the time we were in prison and were never found out. Of course, I had to spend time doing that.

Because of indiscipline under the prison regulations — I had organized a protest one day when Batista visited the prison — I was placed in solitary, and I spent many months alone until, finally, Raúl was sent to share my cell. We continued to be isolated, but there were two of us. It made my situation a little more bearable when they put Raúl in there during the last few months we were in prison.

During that period, I read practically all of the books Dostoevski wrote, though I don't think it's a very good idea to read *The House of the Dead* when you're in prison. I remember that I also read the 10 volumes of Romain Rolland's *Jean-Christophe* and Victor Hugo's *Les Miserables*, which is another long one, but I had read it before. I also read most of Balzac's *Human Comedy*.

I became so interested in Romain Rolland that I read until 11:00 or 12:00 at night, using matches and a lamp I had made that burned cooking oil. I read with the lamp outside my mosquito net. Just imagine how hard it was on my eyes, reading with light that was filtered through a mosquito net!

Later, in Mexico and in the Sierra Maestra mountains, I always had a book of some kind with me. I think I have read all the books ever written, by both sides, about World War II. I've also read a lot throughout the years since the triumph of the Revolution, though not as much as I would like to have read.

At one time, I read piles of books on agriculture; I delved into agriculture and cattle raising, especially pasture and other crops. I must have read and studied 70, 80 or 100 books on agriculture — agricultural techniques and tropical agriculture. I spent a lot of time on some topics.

I've had a selection made of the 250 or 300 best literary works that have been written in Latin America, and we want to print and distribute them throughout the country. I've read some but not all of them. I think this is very important, because, as part of a true policy of integration, we must promote greater knowledge of Latin American history, literature and reality. This is one of the ingredients in the formation of an integrationist awareness in Latin America.

You asked what I've read recently. I've read a little bit of everything. I keep running out of books and having to get more. Last night, I was reading a little novel called *Perfume*, by Patrick Süskind. It's an unusual subject, very interesting and pleasant. I have around 30 pages to go, and I don't know how it's going to end. I'm at the part where the French nobleman is trying to protect his redheaded daughter from the dangers involved in the activities of the main character, the perfume maker Grenouille. That's the last book I've been reading.

I've also read a lot about construction and other subjects related to my daily work, but you asked about other kinds of books. I've always liked literature and have my favorite authors.

I've read all of García Márquez's books, I think, and a lot of other Latin American literature, though I still have much to read. I've even promoted a collection of the best Latin American literary works since the 1920s. In a way, Latin American literature has been greatly influenced politically since the October Revolution — for the good.

Several days ago, I was reading some books on ancient Rome, ancient Greece, ancient times, the Chinese and the Aztecs. At the same time, I've been rereading — I'm around three quarters of the way through — a thick volume of the writings of Bernal Díaz del Castillo, delving into the great heroism and feats of the Mexican Indians in their resistance to the Spanish conquistadores.

I'm in the midst of that, and, the deeper I go into events

related to the heroism of the Mexican Indians, the more impressed I am. For example, the resistance of Tenochtitlán is something that has no parallel in history; I don't remember any other siege in antiquity to match it, and there were plenty of sieges and battles back then. But a battle waged under such difficult conditions as the one in which Cuauhtémoc, heading the Aztecs, defended the city of Tenochtitlán against a technologically more developed civilization was a fabulous thing: against much more modern weapons; against cannon, guns, crossbows and all that; against the steel they had. I've always been saddened by the conquest, but this part of history makes you feel proud. Well, I'm amazed that nobody has spoken or written more about this, that nobody has made any movies about the Aztecs' resistance.

So, right now, I'm reading three or four books, but the latest one is by the author I mentioned, a work of fiction. I have one waiting for me called *Death is a Lonely Business*, by Bradbury, also fiction. Which one I pick up depends on what work I have, the activities I'm involved in. There are times when you want escapist literature to make you forget your problems a little, and you reach for a work of fiction. Süskind's book teaches you a lot. It's incredible what I've learned about perfumes, even about the technology of perfume making. Literature covers a lot of ground. I have many books; some are heavier going than others.

Let's see what other ones I have here. A biography of Suleiman the Magnificent, who extended the Ottoman invasion to the heart of Europe and terrified all the rulers of that era: Francis I, Carlos V and the King of England — Henry VIII, I think it was. But, above all, he had Francis I and Carlos V shaking in their boots with that expansion, and that's another thing I would like to study.

I was recently reading a history of Egypt, of famous Egyptians. Every so often, I go back to the Greek philosophers and am amazed by the things they reasoned out in that era. I like to reread the historians of antiquity: Herodotus, Plutarch, Titus Livius, Xenophon and Suetonius. I keep going back to them. I don't usually read one book at a time; sometimes I'm reading five or six at once, taking them up to suit my mood and how tired I am.

Tomás Borge: It also depends on where they are: one book in one place and another in another.

Fidel Castro: I usually read at home, when I've finished the day's activities and don't have anything else to do. During the day, I read papers — though I don't always read all of them. Chomy knows there's a war on between him and me because of the quantities of papers he gives me every day. There are a lot of them, and they pile up; there are many things to do. That's my bone of contention with Chomy. And then, if there's an important paper to which he hasn't assigned top priority, I protest. I say, "Why didn't you put it in first place? Why didn't you tell me it was on such an important subject?"

Well, now it isn't Chomy; it's another comrade. Now, I have to give him a few lessons — let's put it that way — about my reading habits and my ideas about the quantities of papers I should be given every day. The new man, simply because he's new, is increasing the number of papers. I've noted an increase recently; every day, there are hundreds of them. Of course, the other comrades make a selection, because I couldn't possibly read hundreds of papers every day. Everybody who's done something wants to tell me about it, and then there are the comrades who travel and send in reports. The other comrades assign priorities to the papers that come in every day, and I read the most important ones. Sometimes I get there late at night and have to choose between reading the pile of papers they're left for me or reading a work of literature — and, of course, I choose the book and leave the papers for the morning. So, sometimes, they pile up.

Tomás Borge: If you had to choose one author of fiction as your favorite, who would it be?

Fidel Castro: Cervantes.

Tomás Borge: That was quick.

Fidel Castro: I didn't have to think twice. In that era, literary techniques hadn't been developed. I've read *Don Quixote* five or six times, at least, because of the beauty of Cervantes's subject matter and the way he wrote. The same is true of Cantinflas's movies: I can see them every two or three years, and they seem new to me. Since Cantinflas's movies don't have a story line —

simply a character who couldn't be more engaging — I see them over and over again, and the way he talks and keeps putting his foot in it makes me laugh. Even if I've seen one of Cantinflas's movies more than once, I can go back to it three years later. It's like Chaplin's movies, except that Chaplin's also have content.

Chaplin was a great actor, and his movies have content. Cantinflas's have no content — apart from some sentimental melodrama: a poor, unhappy girl whom he saves or helps to be happy, or a rich woman he falls in love with but who doesn't love him, things like that — but I see them over and over again because of his many faux pas; they make me laugh.

So, I keep going back to Don Quixote, even though there may be modern authors whose technique is better. The only thing I don't like about Cervantes is his insertion of the Arabian stories; sometimes they're quite long and even boring. *Don Quixote* would have been better if he hadn't stuck in the Arabian stories, if it were only about Quixote. Those stories are distracting; it may take 20 minutes to read one of them. Moreover, they're in very small type. That's my only criticism; the work as a whole is simply fabulous.

I've read Shakespeare, but reading a translation from another language isn't the same as reading something in the original Spanish.

Modern writers have lots of technique and write very beautiful things, but they have resources that weren't available to Cervantes. I think he fought in wars against pirates and against the Moors, as they called the Muslims. In Navpaktos, he lost a hand. But what talent! I've read not only *Don Quixote* but also his *Novelas ejemplares* (Exemplary Novels). I liked them very, very much. They're very simply written and pleasing.

Tomás Borge: Who is your favorite poet, Fidel?
Fidel Castro: I like Pablo Neruda very much. He's the one I have read the most and one my favorites, but I like Nicolás Guillén more. I admire Neruda's poetry; it's very beautiful and an inexhaustible source of pleasure, but I like Guillén even more. A little nationalism, chauvinism — I admit it — may be involved here. From classical literature, I learned nearly all of the *Cien*

mejores poesías de la lengua castellana (One Hundred Best Poems in the Spanish Language) by heart. I like the poetry of Martí and Rubén Darío; I think they have an affinity. I like Martí's very much. Even though Martí wasn't primarily a poet, his poetry is pleasing, and I read it with love.

As you see, I don't have much time for reading in all the literary genres.

Tomás Borge: Fidel, do you ever sing?
Fidel Castro: I have a terrible ear for music. I like it, but I don't have the skill.

Tomás Borge: Not even in the shower?
Fidel Castro: No; in the shower, if the water's cold, I sometimes shiver. I don't have that habit, Tomás. Unfortunately, I have a very bad ear for music. I like music very much, especially revolutionary songs, the music of Silvio Rodríguez, Pablito Milanés and Sara González. I'm more familiar with Cuban singers. There's a new one called Enrique Corona who wrote a very stirring song that stays with you. Its lyrics go, "Now is the time to shout 'Revolution!'/Clasp hands with no betwixt -betweens./The best pledge is to do our duty/and know what being Cuban means."

I also like the songs Pablito and Silvio wrote about Nicaragua.

Tomás Borge: Pablito wrote one, and Silvio, another.
Fidel Castro: I've heard both of them, and I like them a lot. I really like that kind of song. I like Carlos Mejía Godoy, a Nicaraguan, and his song to Carlos Fonseca, "Tayacán vencedor de la muerte" (Tayacán, Who Conquers Death). What, exactly, does tayacán mean?

Tomás Borge: It means hero, a brave man.
Fidel Castro: I also liked the singer they murdered in Chile, Víctor Jara.

I like classical music and marches; I have a real soft spot for marches. Of course, I don't have enough time for all these things, and I have to blame nature because it didn't give me musical genes, a good ear for music or a good singing voice. Moreover, I never went to a school where the little aptitude for music there may have been in me could have been developed. I would have liked it very much, but I'll have to wait for my next reincarnation.

Tomás Borge: According to the astrologists, you like marches because you were born on August 13, just as I was... They also say that people born under the sign of Leo march rather than walk.
Fidel Castro: Really?! And we were born on the same day? Do you have a good ear for music?

Tomás Borge: Far from it!
Fidel Castro: Then we're alike, Tomás; it seems that astrology got something right.

But I didn't finish what I was saying. Naturally, I like García Márquez's writing, friendship apart. His works are fabulous, and I think that, when speaking of literature and my favorites in literature, I should mention him.

Tomás Borge: Have you read Cortázar?
Fidel Castro: Not much.

Tomás Borge: You really should read him...
Fidel Castro: All right; thanks for the tip. I'll put him at the top of my list. Which book would you recommend?

Tomás Borge: All of his short stories and his novels *Rayuela* (Hopscotch), *El libro de Manuel* (The Book of Manuel) and *Los premios* (The Awards).
Fidel Castro: He's in the list of authors we selected, of course.

Tomás Borge: Moreover, he was an extraordinary man, an exceptional human being. I was a very close friend of his, and I know what I'm saying.

With your great love of literature, I suppose you have pretty close relations with Cuban writers.
Fidel Castro: With some, but not many.

Tomás Borge: Why?

Fidel Castro: Because of my work. As I told you, I dedicate myself to my work; I'm a slave to it. I don't delegate the things I want to see and do. I like to work. All my life, I have liked it. If I want to see something in agriculture, I go there and see everything related to it, and the same is true of construction and any other activity. But contact with writers hasn't been in the immediate sphere of my work. I have some friends whom I respect and admire a great deal, and I keep in contact with them whenever I can, but I haven't been able to cultivate that, Tomás; my work load hasn't made that possible.

Tomás Borge: Here in Cuba, there's an ongoing resurrection of aesthetics and good literature, with poets and writers of singular sensitivity.

Fidel Castro: There are so many of them it would be impossible to list them all.

Tomás Borge: It wasn't by chance that Abel Prieto has become a member of the Political Bureau [of the Communist Party of Cuba], was it?

Fidel Castro: Abel Prieto became a member not only because he is a capable, prestigious intellectual but also because he is a great revolutionary. They are two separate things. Moreover, he is an individual with leadership ability; he's an extraordinary person. He wasn't elected as an intellectual, though. Rather, he is an outstanding intellectual who is worthy of the leadership task he is carrying out. The better I know him, the more I admire him.

Tomás Borge: In addition, he is a modest, unassuming person. I consider that very important in a revolutionary.

CHAPTER 14

Struggling for utopia means, in part, building it

All of the virtues are attributed to you, Fidel — you, who have filled the pages of all newspapers and magazines, who have been on all screens and have seen the effect your words have on multitudes.

Some of your friends and comrades have told me some amazing anecdotes about your sensitivity, that has survived disillusionment, failure, ingratitude, days of glory, assassination attempts and other people's selling out.

The mother of Camilo Torres once said of you, "He is a man easily moved to tears." People also say that you are the most outstanding person in the modern world. People feel strongly about you: they either hate or love you.

Those who love you consider you blameless. I think, really, that you are, because you never lie, not even when you are authoritarian and stubborn. Those are defects that make you more human. I also think that sometimes you are careless about your clothes, but nobody tells you.

I have the impression that, with more discretion than need be, your comrades don't dare to question some of your opinions, even when they consider them mistaken. However, Fernando Ravelo, Cuba's Ambassador to Nicaragua, says he is sure that different views are expressed in the meetings of the Political Bureau.

According to Carlos Rafael Rodríguez, you have the merit of

listening to those opinions with great attention and of assimilating criticism and suggestions. Our mutual friend, himself a veteran fencer with words, says that you listen, speak, listen and speak, over and over again, until the subject is exhausted and a collective decision has been reached.

It is common for those who are near a leader to imitate them in some way: their voice, their gestures, their style. Nobody imitates you, however, because there is the same distance between you and the others as there was between St. Francis and his friars.

Even those who hate you respect you, and famous writers seek your praise, a glance of recognition. I have seen how the faces of the ordinary people, who sum up the sensitivity of the Latin American peoples who are grateful to Cuba, light up when they approach you to shake your hand.

Many people go up to you, my friend, hoping to say something that will go down in history, yet can barely stammer, "How are you, Fidel? Glad to meet you."

Some people say the most tender and amazing platitudes to you. Others don't say anything at all, because they want to say so much.

You refuse to make your private life public. I think that's correct. However, that silence has given rise to much speculation — most of it fantastic — about beautiful women going into impassioned raptures over you.

Apocalyptic statements credit you with having helped along more of the best and worst events of the last 30 years — the Vietnam War, the liberation of Nicaragua, Watergate, etc., etc., etc. — than any other human being in modern times.

You were in Bogotá during the upheaval in 1948, when Jorge Eliecer Gaitán was assassinated, and took part in an armed raid against Trujillo, defying sharks and stormy seas.

Your life story is yet to be written. It is inevitable that someone will try to portray your private life objectively, no matter how zealously you try to defend what you say is the only thing you possess.

T. B.

Tomás Borge: You warned me, Commander, that you didn't want to break the silence that surrounds some aspects of your private life, and I'm going to respect that.

Fidel Castro: Tomás, you told me you were going to take this up, and I told you what my philosophy was and how I felt about it. Really, the only thing I keep to myself is my private life; I don't have anything more, and it's something I keep as my own preserve. I think that a person's private life shouldn't be used for publicity or politics — as is so commonly done in that capitalist world I detest so much and in that hypocritical world of politicking which I utterly reject. This is the way I think, and I've maintained these views throughout my life. Everybody has their own way of thinking and acting. Let's leave those things to history.

Tomás Borge: I'm convinced I should respect the privacy of your confidence. It has been suggested that political leaders should retire when they turn 60. What do you think of that?

Fidel Castro: If only that were so, Tomás. The problem is a matter not just of retiring, but of being able to retire, which are two different things.

Philosophizing a little on this subject, I would certainly agree with the proponents of the theory that leaders should be as young as possible. I would agree even though, in *The Republic*, Plato said that no person should make themselves responsible for affairs of state until they were 55 and that they should spend the preceding time preparing themselves for assuming important state functions. Life expectancy in Plato's era was 50 or a little less, so, adjusting the figure to allow for our longer life expectancy, I calculate that, in line with Plato's concept, modern humans should be around 80 before they assume functions of state. I think 80 is too old, however.

I would recommend that young people be the ones to carry out revolutions. When I organized the attack on the Moncada Garrison, I was 26. I was 20 or 21 when I joined the Confites Cay expedition to go and free the Dominican Republic from Trujillo's tyranny, and around 21 when I took part in the Bogotá uprising and joined the forces that had rebelled after Gaitán's murder.

When you're 20, 25 or 30, you do things that you can't do when you're 60.

When I was 60, I couldn't have participated in a *Granma* landing or begun a guerrilla struggle in the Sierra Maestra; I couldn't have done what I did then. Perhaps, after our fronts had been set up and organized and we already had a solid nucleus for our army, I could have done it. But, thinking back to what I did between 1956, when I was 30, and the triumph of the Revolution [in January 1959], when I was 32, I think that I couldn't have done the things I did then if I had been as old as I am now. That is, I would recommend being younger for engaging in such tasks.

I think a little more maturity is needed for guiding a state and developing a revolutionary process. I had too little experience when I first exercised the powers of government, but, with the passing of the years, I've gained some. I would say that now I have as much experience as possible on countless aspects and matters, and this is worth quite a lot.

Really, I wish I had the experience I now have together with the youth I had when the Revolution was begun. In these difficult times, that require so much effort, above all, I wish I had that youth, because a lot of energy is required, and I have to make a special effort to do what I'm doing. I do it with great pleasure, but, really, I think it would be much better if I could combine youth and experience.

Moreover — I tell you this frankly — I wish other people could take over my tasks. I carry them out with pleasure, but as a duty — not to satisfy any personal desires. I know my work is useful, and, as long as it is, I must do it for the Revolution. I don't have the energy I had when we were in the mountains or in the early years after the triumph of the Revolution, but I have enough strength to keep on fighting, and, as long as my comrades believe that I'm needed in that battle, that's what I'll do. I'm not satisfying a personal ambition but am simply doing my duty.

Lastly, the matter of age is relative. It depends to a great extent on the person, on their state of health. Some people have to retire while they're still very young because their health doesn't allow them to work; others continue to carry out public functions at 70, 75 and even 80, because their health is good enough for them to do so. It also depends on the tasks. Some tasks are very easy, while others are more difficult. In socialism, in a revolution, the tasks are hard, difficult; a great effort is required. Therefore, you have to give your all and make a great effort to carry out your tasks.

It also depends on a person's motivation. If you don't have very powerful motivation, you couldn't do what I do. It takes very powerful motivation and, above all, a very great need for you to do it.

The modern world has seen a large number of statesmen who were much older than I. My problem isn't age so much as my forgetting that I'm not 30 anymore; that's my problem. My mind is adapted to being 30, and I'm not 30, but 65. Summing up, I think that old people shouldn't be denied the right to engage in political affairs — and I think this is the first time in my life I've referred to myself as an old man.

Tomás Borge: You're the youngest "old man" I've ever met. There is a very widespread idea that may be worth commenting on: "Power tends to corrupt, and absolute power corrupts absolutely." How did you manage not to fall into that trap?

Fidel Castro: I would agree with that statement in principle. I think that power does corrupt — let's call it power, but we could just as well say having important posts, important functions, important responsibilities, which is what is usually called power. I've seen this in people more than once. When I speak of corruption, I include arrogance, lack of humility, and abuses of power. Some people begin to change, to be deformed, as soon as they have a little responsibility — a little, not much, power — and I think that, the more power people have, the greater the risk; that's a fact. I think it requires being aware of the danger and ever alert, ever vigilant against it.

As for me, I have never viewed power as something that is mine, something that is to be enjoyed. Rather, I have looked on power — or authority, as some people like to call it — as the tool of a legitimate cause, of a revolution, of something else I wanted, of a goal I set myself, and I have felt completely identified with the people. I've never lost contact with ordinary men and women.

Throughout my life, ever since I began working, I've worked as an artisan. When we began organizing the Movement, I was a grassroots worker. I didn't delegate the job of recruiting the combatants in the cells — I myself recruited thousands of people and I spoke personally with thousands of them when I was organizing the revolutionary movement. I could do that because I worked perfectly legally when I organized the revolutionary movement.

All my life, since before the March 10, 1952, coup, I worked with people myself, and I kept up that contact all the time: as a university student, when I began to become known as a student leader; later on, as a political leader; and after March 10, 1952, as an organizer of the revolutionary process. I worked like a slave in all those things, personally. Later on, I organized the *Granma* expedition and trained the personnel. During the war, I stayed with the troops the whole 25 months of the war; I stayed with the soldiers and lived like them. I've held on to those habits throughout the more than 30 years since the triumph of the Revolution. I have a lot of contact with the people; I go to the people, and I admire them. I am always aware of the role the people play. The work of one person is a small, modest part of the great work which consists of all these things in which I've participated, in which the men and women of the masses play the key role.

If you're honest, truly honest, you won't be corrupted. If you're unassuming and have a clear understanding of the worth of people and of yourself, you won't be corrupted. I've maintained eternal vigilance about this throughout my life, and I've been very self-critical. I've always examined everything I've done, checking to see whether it was correct or not, whether or not I let myself be carried away, whether or not pride had anything to do with it, and I think I've learned to control myself. "Know thyself" could be another maxim, along with "Always control yourself."

I've harbored these ideas, that are related to the other question you asked me, about history and the role and merits of people. I think this has helped me to remain the same as always, ever since I took my first steps along the path of the Revolution.

You quoted another maxim: "Absolute power corrupts absolutely." I could also subscribe to that, although, really, I haven't had any experience of absolute power, because I've never been in favor of one-person decisions — or, rather, one-person governments.

Ever since we began the Revolution, we had a small leadership nucleus, in two parts: a leadership group composed of several comrades and a three-person executive. That's how we organized the July 26 Movement, recruited people, trained them and set about getting weapons. At the beginning, I was the only "professional" revolutionary. I use this term because I spent all my time in these activities. I didn't have any money, and the other comrades kept me going, paying for my food, rent, gasoline and other things; the comrades paid my bills. That's how I began to be a professional revolutionary, spending all my time in those activities — 15, 16 or 17 hours a day. As I already told you, I did this in the open. That's how we organized everything.

Batista underestimated us; he was worried about other leaders, other political organizations — that had millions of pesos and weapons — and looked down on us, which helped us enormously to do all of our work in the open before the attack on the Moncada Garrison. We did everything in the open, not underground. I'm very glad it was that way, because it was always very difficult for me to work clandestinely — my build was easy to recognize. I could dye my hair or do anything else, but all of my experiences in the underground were always a failure, because I was always recognized immediately. I could only work in the open.

When, after the attack on the Moncada and prison, I had to organize the *Granma* expedition, I went abroad and did it from there. After we returned, I never worked clandestinely again.

Tomás Borge: What about when you were in Mexico?
Fidel Castro: I was discreet, not clandestine.

I was explaining about absolute power, Tomás. Right from the beginning, we had a leadership group, though the comrades gave me many powers, for they had complete confidence in me and I had a lot of authority. I had great authority throughout the process, ever since we began. After the attack on the Moncada, when we reorganized the movement under another name — from then on, it was called the July 26 Movement — we established a National Leadership, and it functioned while I was in prison. I was a part of it, but the other members of the National Leadership who weren't in prison acted with great autonomy.

The National Leadership continued to exist while I was in Mexico. I was a part of it, but the National Leadership in Cuba acted with great autonomy, as those of us who were in Mexico did, too.

An army needs a chief; there's a chief, a commander in chief of a military force in every war. When the war began, I was commander in chief. That's where my title of Commander in Chief came from, because I wasn't a colonel, general, marshal or anything like that, and I haven't been promoted. I've never been promoted in more than 30 years. I'm still a commander, and the comrades call me Commander in Chief. I think that, later on, they passed a law turning my rank into a higher one, but I'm still called Commander in Chief — not general in chief, or field marshal or anything of that order.

I haven't been promoted since I returned aboard the *Granma*. I was the chief of the military forces; I had that responsibility. But there was still a National Leadership of the Movement, and our army was subordinated to the Movement. Therefore, throughout the war, there was a National Leadership of the July 26 Movement, and its members, most of whom were in the cities and on the plains, had great powers and great autonomy and made countless decisions.

When the Revolution triumphed, we had the Movement with its leaders, plus other organizations: the Popular Socialist Party and the Revolutionary Directorate. Naturally, the July 26 Movement was immensely more powerful than the others, but we didn't take a sectarian attitude — far from it. We invited them to share in the authority and shared power with the other revolutionary organizations. Right from the start, we created a National Leadership for coordinating activities, and, when the organizations merged, we created a Central Committee. That is, we organized a leadership group. Since the Revolution, we have always had a leadership group, and it has always functioned. The main, key, decisive things have always been discussed collectively in the Central Committee or in the Political Bureau. I don't make one-person decisions about basic, very important things.

Now, I do have a sphere of activity, a series of prerogatives, a sphere of action for many things about which I can make decisions, just as everybody has powers here. In a socialist, revolutionary process, people have a lot of powers in their spheres of action.

The party and government leaders have many powers in a municipality; the management of a factory has many powers there; the leaders of a province have many powers, and so do the leaders of a ministry. I have certain powers in the Executive Committee and Political Bureau. The Central Committee is more important than the Political Bureau, but, of course, it doesn't meet daily; as a norm, it meets twice a year.

The National Assembly has the greatest constitutional powers, but it doesn't remain in session throughout the year. Between sessions, the Council of State must approve legislative decrees and other important legislative decisions. The Council of State has certain important powers when the National Assembly isn't in session.

All my life, right from the beginning, I have promoted group decisions — never one-person decisions. I've had a very clear, very precise understanding of this, and it has protected me against what might be called any form of absolute power.

Great authority, yes. I don't deny that I've had very great authority in all of those organizations — great authority within the group — but basic decisions are analyzed and discussed in depth; I don't make them unilaterally. I pay a lot of attention to the views of the others. Several times they have done things I didn't agree with, but I have always respected the views of the majority of the members of the leadership bodies. I could give you some examples. In general, however, I seek consensus. We don't often make decisions by taking a vote; usually, when there is broad consensus, all the rest of us abide by the views of the majority, even though we may not agree with them completely. This doesn't involve matters of principle; it's for tactical matters and tactical decisions. If, someday, there were to be disagreement over a matter of principle, that would be a problem, a kind of crisis. But that kind of thing hasn't happened yet in our Revolution, and we've always sought consensus. That's the way we have made basic decisions.

Tomás Borge: You say there's no cult of the personality in Cuba?
Fidel Castro: That's right. There are things that may be associated with what I was just telling you. And one of those is the question of cult of the personality. Absolute powers are usually accompanied by certain attributes, but, in a country such as this, it's very difficult for there to be any form of absolute power, because Cubans discuss and analyze everything — baseball, agriculture, politics, everything. Cubans discuss everything; that's part of our character.

The history of our country prior to the Revolution is full of vain politicians. However, one of the first things we did after the triumph of the Revolution — and the conditions were ripe for enormous personal power, but I never let myself be tempted or swayed by that — one of the Revolution's first laws (I wonder if others have done this anywhere else) was to prohibit official portraits.

In Cuba, in more than 30 years of the Revolution, there have never been any official pictures. Every so often, a visitor, a friend, a foreigner or a Cuban asks me for a picture. The pictures of me that people may have in their homes are taken from magazines and posters for national meetings. None of the pictures of me that the people have are official ones; they are pictures they have cut out of publications. Sometimes, people have asked, "Please send me a picture," and I've looked for one and sent it to them. But there isn't any official picture in Cuba; that was prohibited in the first few months after the triumph of the Revolution.

Another thing: we absolutely forbade naming schools, institutions and other installations after living people; they can be named only after people who are dead. Lastly, we don't allow statues, busts or other things like that to be put up in honor of living people. No streets or schools — nothing — may be named after living revolutionaries, nor may there be any statues or busts of living revolutionaries. That was one of the first measures the Revolution took, back in 1959, when the subject of cult of the personality hadn't come up yet in the Soviet Union or those other places. In fact, the term "cult of the personality" began to take on its present connotation after the triumph of the Cuban Revolution, when we had already taken all those measures.

I've always spoken out against all manifestations of a cult or adulation of leaders. We established that tradition. Even the military ranks of our comrades in the Rebel Army never rose above commander, and we had to invent new intermediary ranks so we wouldn't exceed it.

For many years, the ranks we had were captain, first captain, major, commander and first commander; we had an enormous army but no generals, and all of those units didn't fit into the few ranks we had, in which the highest was commander. Then, one day, we were forced to use higher ranks because of our relations with the other socialist countries and many other countries, too — because nobody understood our nomenclature of commander on down. Who had similar ranks in the other armies? One day, we had to leave sentimentality behind and accept the ranks of colonel and general and even several ranks of general: brigadier general, major general, lieutenant general and general. However, I had the privilege of retaining the original name of my rank, and I wasn't promoted — at least, I wasn't promoted in terms of my title. I kept on being a commander — in this case, Commander in Chief, which, as I said, was made into a rank by law. I've been very careful in all these matters and have always been unassuming. It seems to me that that has been a key factor in my being able to maintain the integrity of the early days when I began being a revolutionary.

Tomás Borge: I'm commander, too; I'm very pleased that I have the same rank as you.

How do you see yourself? Do you wish you hadn't done some of the things you did in your life? Do you feel fulfilled?
Fidel Castro: I've made tactical mistakes; I wish I hadn't made them. I already told you about my tactical mistake that was responsible for the setback at Alegría de Pío on December 5, 1956.

I wish I hadn't made any tactical mistakes. But I haven't made any strategic mistakes in the course of the Revolution; I haven't ever gone against principles. Therefore, I don't have any cause for remorse.

As for my decision to do what I have done, I'll never be sorry about that. If I had it to do over, I'd take the same revolutionary path again.

I can't feel entirely satisfied with what I have done; I will always feel I could have done better. Still, I know that we — not just I, but all Cuban revolutionaries, the Cuban people — have done something worthwhile.

Tomás Borge: How would you define the Cuban essence, about which Cuban poets have written so much? Put another way, what does being a Cuban mean to you?

Fidel Castro: Right now, it's something that I value more than ever. I've always placed humankind above homeland. I am an internationalist, first and foremost, without ceasing to be a patriot. But now, when our homeland embodies the highest virtues of a nation — the highest virtues of a noble, combative, heroic people — and of internationalism; when it is confronting the imperialists in an unprecedented, unparalleled gesture; when it has become the front line in the defense of Latin America; and when it is what Martí wanted to make it on the eve of his death at Dos Ríos, a line of defense against "the brutal and turbulent North" — now, when our homeland symbolizes all that, it is not only a source of pride but, for me, a greater privilege than ever to be a Cuban. I have very great esteem — not for the land, this isn't love of the land — and love for my people who live in this land. Martí said:

> Love of homeland, mother,
> Isn't ridiculous love of the land
> Or of the grass under our plants;
> It is invincible hatred of those who oppress it,
> Eternal animosity toward those who attack it.

For me, "homeland" means the people, and I have tremendous, ever-growing admiration for our people, because our people constantly improve. These are the people who both carried out and have been shaped by the Revolution. I love and admire these people, whom I know so well and to whom I feel so closely tied and so committed. I am proud to be a part of them, a son of these people.

Tomás Borge: Many of us have dreamed of founding utopias. Do you think it's worthwhile for us to keep on dreaming of a better world in humanity's present conditions and circumstances?

Fidel Castro: We have no alternative. We must continue dreaming, with the hope that the better world will become a reality — as it will, if we keep struggling. Humanity should never renounce its dreams, its utopias. Struggling for utopia means, in part, building it.

Martí also said that today's dreams were tomorrow's reality. In my country, we have seen many of the dreams of the past, a great part of our utopias, become reality. And, since we have seen this, we have the right to keep on dreaming of things that will become realities someday, both in our country and in the world as a whole. If we didn't think this way, we would have to stop struggling, for the only logical conclusion would be to abandon the struggle, and I think that a revolutionary never abandons the struggle, just as they never stop dreaming.

CHAPTER 15

A kernel of corn

Tomás Borge: Fidel, I'd like you to accept membership in the Council of Friends of the Green Smile, a foundation we created in Nicaragua to care for indigent families and for sad, emaciated, abandoned children who beg and clean windshields. We want to involve the children in the struggle to protect nature, and we select outstanding people from all over the world to join in this exercise of tenderness.

Fidel Castro: Tomás, I feel very honored by your invitation to be a friend of that noble institution you're promoting. Naturally, I accept and will cooperate as much as I can with that effort.

Tomás Borge: Brother, we've just completed a three-day stint. The least I can do is express my gratitude for your patience and expressions of affection and for your having enabled me to have this dream of publishing our talk.

Fidel Castro: It's been a great pleasure to spend these hours answering your questions. I have tried to do so as well and extensively as possible. If I have gone on a bit, I hope you will excuse me. I've really enjoyed talking with you.

Tomás Borge: I think that the quality and length of what you said was correct, and I'm sure it will clear up some misunderstandings.

Fidel Castro: Some of the misunderstandings. I couldn't go into everything, but at least I have set forth my thinking on some topics. I've told you some things I hadn't said before.

I really do have a lot of work. As I said, I dedicate myself to work and don't limit myself to strategic matters; sometimes I also take care of the details, and I have a lot of work right now. I have had many requests for interviews and I have tried not to commit myself, because, if I were to give all the interviews I'm asked to, I would have to spend all my time on them, and I can't do that. But I had to agree to your request.

Tomás Borge: Your words should help to clear away some of the gray mists that political pornography has invented to hide simple, straightforward truths.

In my opinion, Fidel, you hold a place in history as a knight errant, clothed in the armor of intelligence and courage as well as determination and humility.

I think that you're more interested in growing prize tomatoes, spurring genetics and further reducing Cuba's already impressively low infant mortality rate than in measuring your achievements against that glory-packed kernel of corn.

What I have seen convinces me of your joy when men, women and children come up to you, even to express a gentle reproach for your not having visited a school or a factory, and of your commitment to go there someday — promises that they know you will keep.

Over the years — we have known each other for more than a decade, now — I have seen you take an interest in such day-to-day matters as the results of a sports competition, the lightness of wine and the miracles of fibers in health. I have seen you laugh, cry, be amazed by ingratitude, push grudges aside, and become indignant over villainy, selfishness, corruption and arrogance.

I want to reiterate that I am not impartial, for my feelings and convictions are with you, on this side of the frontier. For several hours I was a journalist, but I never stopped being a comrade, a friend.

I am impressed by the clear organization of your ideas and by your sincerity. I am convinced that I have spoken with a true disciple of Martí, a standard for that kernel of corn.

Index

Also published by Ocean Press

Fidel and Malcolm X — Memories of a meeting
by Rosemari Mealy
The first extensive account of the 1960 encounter between Fidel
Castro and Malcolm X in Harlem's Hotel Theresa. With
testimonies from contemporaries of both figures, the story is told
of the stay in Harlem of Castro and the Cuban delegation after
they were forced from a downtown Manhattan hotel. Previously
unpublished photos are included, along with Amiri Baraka's
(LeRoi Jones) award-winning 1959 essay "Cuba Libre".
80 pages plus 16 pages photos, chronology
ISBN paper 1-875284-67-2

Tomorrow is too late — Development and the environmental crisis in the Third World
by Fidel Castro
During the most controversial and widely discussed speech to the
1992 World Earth Summit in Rio, Cuban President Fidel Castro
caught the imagination of the summit's delegates when he cast
blame for the world's environmental crisis on Western consumer
societies and called for the use of science to sustain development
without pollution. Comprising Castro's speech and the full text of
the document he prepared for the delegates — both printed in
English for the first time — this book presents the international
environmental crisis in a new and important perspective.
56 pages
ISBN paper 1-875284-73-7

Can Cuba survive?
An interview with Fidel Castro
by Beatriz Pagés
In a frank exchange with Mexican journalist Beatriz Pagés, Cuban
leader Fidel Castro confronts the realities of Cuba in a "new
world order" and accepts the challenge to answer the most
controversial question: Can Cuba survive?
105 pages
ISBN paper 1-875284-58-3

Also published by Ocean Press

Island in the storm —
The Cuban Communist Party's fourth congress
by Gail Reed
Island in the storm describes Cuba's strategy for survival, as it
emerged from the most critical meeting in the revolution's
history. This volume contains the unedited texts of all Congress
resolutions, Fidel Castro's first detailed disclosure of the state of
the Cuban economy and biographies of the new Cuban
leadership.
200 pages plus 16 pages photos
ISBN paper 1-875284-48-6

The Cuban Revolution and the United States —
A chronological history
by Jane Franklin
An invaluable resource for scholars, teachers, journalists,
legislators, and anyone interested in international relations, this
volume offers an unprecedented vision of Cuban-U.S. relations.
Cuba watchers will wonder how they got along without it.

Based on exceptionally wide research, this history provides a
day-by-day, year-by-year report of developments involving Cuba
and the United States from January 1, 1959, through 1990. An
introductory section, starting with the arrival of Christopher
Columbus in the Caribbean, chronicles the events that led to the
triumph of the revolution in Cuba in 1959.

Indispensable as a reference guide, *The Cuban Revolution and
the United States* is also an eye-opening narrative, interrelating
major crises with seemingly minor or secret episodes.

Published in association with the Center for Cuban Studies.
276 pages plus 8 pages photos
ISBN paper 1-875284-26-5